LETTERS FROM SIDE LAKE

A Chronicle of Life in the North Woods

PETER M. LESCHAK

PERENNIAL LIBRARY

Harper & Row, Publishers, New York

Cambridge, Philadelphia, San Francisco, Washington
London, Mexico City, São Paulo, Singapore, Sydney

Portions of this work originally appeared in somewhat different form in *TWA Ambassador, Minnesota Monthly,* and *Twin Cities.*

Grateful acknowledgment is made for permission to reprint the following:

Material originally appearing in *Twin Cities,* © 1984, 1985 Dorn Communications, Inc. Reprinted with permission of *Twin Cities.*
Lines from "Song of Amergin" from *The White Goddess,* by Robert Graves. Copyright 1948 by International Authors N. V., © renewed 1976 by Robert Graves. Reprinted by permission of Farrar, Straus & Giroux, Inc., A. P. Watt Ltd., and the Executors of the Estate of Robert Graves.

A hardcover edition of this book is published by Harper & Row, Publishers, Inc.

First PERENNIAL LIBRARY edition published 1988.

Designer: Charlotte Staub
Copyeditor: Katherine G. Ness

Library of Congress Cataloging-in-Publication Data

Leschak, Peter M.
   Letters from Side Lake.

   "Perennial Library."

   1. Side Lake Region (Minn. : Lake)—Social Life and customs.   2. Country life—Minnesota—Side Lake Region (Lake)   3. Leschak, Peter M.   4. Side Lake Region
(Minn. : Lake—Biography.   I. Title.
F612.S25L47   1988   977.6'77   86-46081
ISBN 0-06-097167-3 (pbk.)

88 89 90 91 92 FG 10 9 8 7 6 5 4 3 2 1

Letters from Side Lake

For Pam.
Without her confidence,
competence, and encouragement,
this book would not
have come to pass.

CONTENTS

I'd like to thank the following editors for the opportunities they offered and the editing they performed: D. J. Tice and Bonnie Blodgett at Paulsen Publishing, Diane Hellekson and Jeff Johnson at *Minnesota Monthly*, and Dan Kelly at *Twin Cities*.

Letters from Side Lake

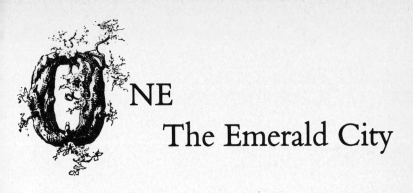

ONE
The Emerald City

How many times have you seen the movie *The Wizard of Oz*? Well, I recently saw it yet again, and the old magic has tarnished only a little. Once again I enjoyed watching my favorite scene (besides the Munchkin town, that is): Dorothy and her odd menagerie of companions have just emerged from the gloomy forest, and across a vast and enchanting field of flowers they can see the magnificent Emerald City, the focus of all their hopes and dreams. For them it is a joyous moment, filled with happy expectations.

But since I know the story, it is a bittersweet moment for me. I know they will be betrayed there, disappointed in their quest for what they think the City promises. Of course everything turns out okay in the end, but I'm sure you'll recall that (a) Dorothy ends up back on a hog farm in Kansas and (b) the whole thing was just a dream in the first place.

So, as I watch Dorothy and Toto et al. skip along the Yellow Brick Road toward the Emerald City, I experience a strange sensation of déjà vu. Hey, I did that! Only I wasn't skipping, I was slouched in the seat of a Greyhound bus; the road was black asphalt, not golden brick; and the city was Minneapolis–St. Paul (MSP to those who, like the winged monkeys of the Wicked Witch of the West, flew in).

The year was 1969, and I was headed from a small mining town on the Mesabi Iron Range in northern Minnesota to seek the promise and the power of *The Cities*. The whole spectrum of society, from Mom to Howdy Doody, from teachers to preachers, from textbooks to comic books, had urged me, either overtly or subtly, to "Follow the Yellow Brick Road!" I was to leave the sticks and enter the Emerald City. There was a wizard there, in the guise of a college education, and it would open all the doors "if I only had a brain."

But it was not to be—even though, on the best evidence, I did have a brain. I think the trouble started on the bus. Taking the bus was a shade more romantic in those days. After all, Paul Simon and "Kathy" boarded a bus to go off looking for America, and Simon prefaced the odyssey with an invitation to "let us be lovers." From his seat on the bus he witnessed a fateful moonrise which initiated a journey to the depths of his soul ("Kathy, I'm lost").

Nevertheless, my bus ride was a non-event. No existential insights, no quests, and certainly no Kathy. It was just mundane transportation from point A to point B. But my pulse rate rose as we cruised into the center city. It was like arriving on the surface of an alien planet. I could hear Dorothy say: "Well, Toto, I guess we're not in Kansas anymore."

I climbed into a cab at the bus depot and said to the driver, "The College of St. Thomas, please," expecting him to nod his head authoritatively and drive right off. But he hesitated, and I was startled. "Is that," he asked, "over on Cleveland?"

He was asking *me*? Hey, we were talking wizards here. Did Dorothy have to tell the gatekeeper of the Emerald City where to find the Wizard? At a loss, I just said "Yes," and hoped for the best. As it turned out, Cleveland was correct, but I felt uneasy that the cabbie hadn't been sure. Weren't they supposed to *know*? Was I harboring other illusions about the city?

Yes and no. I expected The Cities to be a little crazy, but I was taken aback when I encountered the craziness firsthand. In quick succession, I had a series of experiences which left me off balance.

I was waiting for a bus at a corner on Wabasha Street, a main St. Paul thoroughfare not far from the capitol. It was a blustery January evening, definitely parka weather. The bus arrived and the doors snapped open. Out hopped a man clad only in pajamas and slippers. He had a newspaper tucked under one arm and was the picture of nonchalance as he strolled off down the street. I was amazed, not so much at the man himself as at the reaction of the other people at the stop. That is to say, there was no reaction; nary a titter nor a snort. That struck me as very odd. Were pajama-clad bus riders (in winter) that commonplace? If so, why, and did I really want to know?

Shortly thereafter, I was strolling in Nicollet Mall, in downtown Minneapolis, on a fine Sunday afternoon when I was approached by an older woman who exuded wealth. She had on a splendid, stunning fur coat and was veritably dripping with jewelry. Her hair and makeup gave the impression of being professionally done, and I could just picture her stepping out of a limousine about two blocks long. She looked rich, powerful, and distinguished, and I was astonished when she asked me if I could give her 35 cents for bus fare. She said she was broke and she needed to go see her sister who was dying of cancer, etc., etc. I was embarrassed to discover I had no money on me (a common condition in those college days), and I told her so. I could tell she didn't believe me. Isn't it curious, I thought, that here was a rich woman begging for coins, and I was the one who was embarrassed. And disoriented.

Later the same week when I was hitchhiking on Hamline Avenue (a bus strike was in progress), I was picked up by a guy in a Volkswagen who looked to be about my age. We were making pleasant small talk when he abruptly made an explicit homosexual proposition. I said, "What!," and instead of taking it as a shocked exclamation, he treated it as an expression of curiosity and began to explain precisely what he meant. I informed him that I was aware of what he was talking about, and that he could let me out at the next intersection. All the way there (a whole half block!), I wondered what the hell I was going to do if he didn't stop. Fortunately he did, and I was content to walk the rest of the way.

All these incidents were trivial, but often it's the little things that have the biggest impact. Earthshaking events tend to slide off the surface of the brain and become a part of history before we have the time to digest them. Besides, they rarely happen to *you*. It's the odd look or innocuous comment on Monday afternoon that leaves the indelible impression.

For instance, there was the time in Spanish class when a classmate, a city boy born and bred, was asked to say, in Spanish of course, what he thought of when he heard the word "arbol" (tree). Immediately he responded with "parque" (park). I was surprised. What about "bosque" (forest)? Was the man so out of touch (or was I?) that "tree" meant merely a park? Why did that upset me? To associate a tree with a park before a forest would never have occurred to me. Were we that different? Did it matter? Did forests matter, in the city? If not, did I belong there? If the instructor had said "ave" (bird), would the student have said "aeropuerto" (airport)? I shuddered to think of it.

But then, maybe, like the Cowardly Lion, I simply lacked courage. The courage to face a new world, a rapidly paced and changing world where all the big things were happening. Could I carve out a niche here? There was reason to wonder. There were a million things going on, a banquet of possibilities: "Seek and ye shall find."

And we did seek. My dorm-mates and I were all small-town or rural boys, and the impression we had of The Cities was that of a sparkling array of social, cultural, educational, and sporting events. The only catch was that they usually required money. Not an awful lot, but we had none. Just attending college was a burden. We found there is nothing more boring than being broke in the city. When we had time for "recreation" we were often reduced to wandering along Lake Street, ogling girls and counting Corvettes (the record was eleven in two minutes). It was depressing, cumulatively so, and we reached the nadir one cold night in February.

We were walking across the Lake Street Bridge after another evening filled with nothing, when I guess I went a little crazy (I should have worn pajamas). Without a word to my startled companions, I climbed over the guardrail and lowered myself down onto the steel support members of the bridge. Grasping the bottom of an icy girder, I slid my legs off it and dangled there, close to one hundred feet above the freezing Mississippi.

"Are you out of your mind!" yelled one of my friends, visibly nervous.

"Probably," I replied, "but guess what? I'm not bored."

At that, one of the others joined me, and we hung there for a few moments like oversized, demented bats.

We obviously needed to get a few things into perspective, as the Munchkins did for instance. Did you ever notice that while they all clamored for Dorothy to "Follow the Yellow Brick Road," not one of them ventured to do likewise? They had a handle on their world and the last thing they needed to do was to start fooling around with wizards and other dubious folk.

I thought I was slowly getting a handle on city life when at lunch one day I met a student who was from Manhattan. (He never offered a convincing explanation for his presence at St. Thomas.) In the course of our chit-chat I mentioned, in a wistful way, how nice it was going to be to head home during the next semester break and slip out into the woods.

"The woods?" he queried, looking about. "I thought we *were* in the woods!" There was no trace of irony in his voice.

Well, that did it. If there existed a species of human being (mutants, no doubt) that could sincerely consider the Twin Cities the boondocks, then I was nowhere near the end of the Yellow Brick Road, and this was only the beginning of sorrows. For the umpteenth time I had to ask myself: What am I doing in the City? What? Oh yeah, that's right—getting an education.

But "they," that is, everyone, had neglected to tell "us," that is, the "baby boom" cohorts, about a critical bit of demographic data. Simply put, there were too many of us, tens of millions of kids just like me, off to see the wizard. This became apparent when I visited the campus of the University of Minnesota. It resembled nothing if not a gigantic anthill teeming with scrambling students. In a few years this situation, replicated nationwide, would yield curious fruit: Ph.D.'s dumping garbage, sweeping streets, and so on. Many of them, no doubt, were in Manhattan.

The next night I had a dream. I was standing on the Lake Street Bridge, facing north. It was snowing heavily and all the lights of the Cities were obscured. Suddenly the bridge began to dissolve and come apart beneath me, but I wasn't alarmed. I was drifting down through the air, wafting to and fro like a snowflake. I reached the river and eased into the water, but somehow remained dry. As I swam toward the bank, which was covered by a thick blanket of snow, I caught sight of a pair of snowshoes sticking out of a drift. They were mine. Joyfully, I put them on and started shoeing off toward home.

It was, of course, prophetic. At the end of the school year I left St. Thomas, brain and all, never to return. I got back on the Greyhound bus, not even wanting it to be romantic. If I had seen "Kathy," I would have told her to stay away from folk singers. As for me, I would avoid wizards and Emerald Cities. And I did. For a long time I renounced civilization as we know it. By way of rationalized afterthought, I decided what I hadn't liked about the city was the noise, the smell, and the lights. It sounded good (prudent and provincial), and it was even true as far as it went, but it wasn't the chief cause for my disenchantment.

The real reason was simple, but hard to swallow. Hard, because the city was where the action was, where our generation would take up the mantle and march into the future. Our mandate, our responsibility, our glory: all were to be found in the city. The kids who stayed home ended up in the mines, raised kids of their own, and told *them* to go to the city. Hard thoughts. But I couldn't stay in the city. Reason? Simple: I didn't belong there.

So, after five years, a degree, and some wandering, I ended up back in the north.woods where I do belong, not begrudging anyone the promise of the Emerald City nor looking askance at any tree lover who hangs around in parks. The Yellow Brick Road goes both ways. Every time I don my snowshoes I'm reminded of the Lake Street Bridge. But the shoes of that long-ago dream now hang on a solid log wall. Raising those logs was a kind of baptism, and I won't be telling you any more city stories.

TWO

Log Walls, Big Dipper

Returning home was a tricky business. I had idealized the land, fondly recalling things as they never really were. Outdoor scenes were not as brilliant as imagined in vivid Technicolor on a drab and rainy metropolitan afternoon.

It could have been disappointing, but I had a new perspective. It was Pam's, and through her eyes I could see northern Minnesota as something new. She was born and raised in Louisiana, and we'd been married for less than a year when I returned home to live in the woods. We arrived in late December, a few days before a wicked blizzard, the worst in a decade, lashed the land and buried us.

Pam had never seen more than a few inches of transient southern snow, a harmless, fun-filled novelty item. Through her amazement I was reacquainted with the disdainful but exciting power of a northern winter storm—the delicious helplessness as drifts climb up to the windows and the air turns pure white, saturated with gusty snow.

After two days of blank howling, the sky cleared from the northwest, bright blue and bitterly cold. Arctic drafts pushed in from Canada, and Pam breathed −20 degree air for the first time. The experience was brief. She would prefer a good Gulf Coast hurricane, she said. I replied that the cold was invigorating, a stimulus for longevity, and anyway, the winters only lasted until April. She wondered if self-defense was grounds for divorce.

Nevertheless we soon rented a secluded farmhouse fifteen miles from town and tried to snuggle in for the rest of the winter. It was an old house, and a little creepy. We didn't know that Leon had died beneath our cellar steps.

The basement did seem a bit strange from the start. It was divided into three small rooms, each dank and dirty. One room was all but filled by an ancient coal furnace, like a great octopus with its maze of ductwork. The room, black with coal dust, seemed to suck up light, and when you opened the firebox door to stoke the acrid orange-blue flames, the shadow of your shoveling danced, black on black, against the cold rock and cement walls. In the spring, melting snow and heavy rains sent water seeping through the wall in one corner. Listening to it drip, you could easily imagine that you were in a mine shaft.

A second room had only a partial concrete floor, half of it having been left in dirt. It was littered with what we took to be fossilized cat droppings. The third room, at first glance, seemed more like a normal basement. Against one wall stood shelves loaded with mason jars, tools, and old newspapers; along another leaned a stack of scrap lumber and miscellaneous household items common to basements everywhere. Still, there was something odd about that room, and after a few trips down there we realized what it was. The room should have been larger—there was more house overhead than basement below. Soon we noticed that behind the shelves there had once been a door, a doorway that had been plastered over and sealed. It was right out of Poe—"For the love of God, Montressor!"

By hoisting myself to the top of the wall and peering between the joists, I could see that there was indeed another room, about ten feet by twelve. It had been filled with dirt, and then mortared shut. Our landlord, who had only recently purchased the property, had noticed this oddity, too, but had no explanation.

Busy with new jobs and winter chores, Pam and I quickly forgot about our curious cellar. Then, one bitterly cold night about a month after we had moved in, we drove down to the local tavern, the better to fight off the deep-winter blues. We got to talking with a local man, born and bred in the area. He perked up considerably when we told him where we were living. "Hey," he announced, "my grandfather committed suicide in that house!"

No one likes to hear such things about the place where they sleep, but once told, it is impossible to resist the gory details. Our new friend was eager to oblige. It seems that one day, some years earlier, grandfather Leon decided to shoot his wife. His intentions became clear to the unfortunate woman and her daughter, and as Leon went to fetch his rifle, the two women fled from the house and out across an open field. Pursuing them, Leon drew a bead on his wife and squeezed the trigger, and just then his daughter stumbled and fell. Neither woman was hurt, but Leon, believing that he had shot his daughter, slithered under the basement steps and blew his brains out.

It was an ideal scenario for a haunted house. A wretched person, torn by unspeakable grief and guilt, murders himself in a grisly manner, seeking the peace of death. Of course, it doesn't work. The disembodied soul, tormented in the next world, seeks relief by haunting the place of his last residence on earth. Leon was the perfect spectral candidate, and few places I've ever seen could match that basement as an abode for a restless poltergeist.

Neither Pam nor I believe in ghosts, but even so we returned home slightly spooked. Before retiring, I descended the cellar steps to stoke the old furnace for the night. I was nervous and skittish, and angry at myself for being so. Summoning my courage, I paused to kneel and peer beneath those steps. Little light penetrated the dusty, cobwebbed recess where Leon had breathed his last, but as my eyes became accustomed to the gloom I could make out a dark stain against the concrete wall. Blood? We went to bed shortly thereafter, both trying to forget about Leon.

A few hours later, well after midnight, we were awakened by a single gunshot. We bolted upright in bed, wide-eyed and staring at each other. No, it couldn't be. I switched on a lamp to break the spell of sudden fear. "Must've been a tree cracking with the cold," I said. (You've heard that one before. Just prior to the victim's death he is heard to remark, "It's only the wind.") I went into the next room and checked the thermometer. It was 30 degrees below zero outside.

"Had to be a tree popping," I said. It was certainly cold enough. Before returning to bed, I looked at the dark wooden door that led to the cellar. It wouldn't hurt to stoke the furnace, but the idea of going down those creaky stairs with my bare legs exposed to the blackness beneath them gave me pause. Yes, it was a tree cracking, I thought, a loud report that is common on frigid winter nights. Yes, but. If there had been a heavy tread on the steps and the doorknob had turned, I'd have been terrified, but not surprised.

I became angry. My fear was ridiculous. Since I was up and so cold, I really should feed the fire. Yes, but. I went back to the bedroom and got our .410 shotgun. That, of course, was completely illogical. If there was some sort of supernatural manifestation in our basement, what good would a gun do me? No matter. The stock of the weapon felt warm cradled in the crook of my arm. My finger played around the trigger guard as I opened the door to the cellar, flicked on the dim stairwell light, and slowly descended toward the blackness below. The skin crawled on the back of my calves, but no gnarled, bony hand clawed at them from Leon's cul-de-sac. I edged into the darkened furnace room, muzzle first, and flipped on another light. Nothing was lurking there, either.

I shoveled three or four scoops of coal into the firebox and hurried back upstairs. On the way I glanced beneath the steps, and of course saw only cobwebs. I returned to bed and we slept peacefully.

The morning sun rendered the night's fears impotent, but not forgotten. That afternoon, when I returned home from work, I installed a dead-bolt lock on the basement door. I told Pam that it would be easy for someone to break into the house through the coal bin, that we needed the extra security, and she agreed. But we both knew the lock was for Leon.

As one part of my mind was easily possessed by irrational fears, so another part was easily comforted by irrational precautions. I don't believe in ghosts, but I do believe in fear, and for the price of a cheap lock I exorcised Leon. His dark memory never troubled us again, even when the wind howled and birches moaned in the cold.

But that house was another reason to acquire our own, though we hardly needed more motivation. It was our first goal to-gether—to have our own place, built with our own hands.

The back-to-the-land revival had followed hard on the up-heavals of the 1960s, and our generation seemed to be migrating to the fields and forests en masse, Mother's Lifers bound for organic glory; for communion with Nature, neighbors, and themselves. But it was an illusion. Many were called (though not a majority) but few were chosen. The rural Yellow Brick Road was rough. It could rip out the transmission of your Firebird (which, in any case, was a poor vehicle for hauling hay and goats). More lip service was paid than dues. But we were deter-mined to succeed in the woods, and Pam found the forty acres we needed.

She had landed a job as a reporter for the *Hibbing Daily Tribune,* and in the course of covering the governmental activity of a neighboring county, she met the local land commissioner. She asked him if he knew of any decent acreage for sale, and he replied that as a matter of fact, he owned forty forested acres in the Side Lake area, and we could have them for $5000.

It sounded worth investigating. It was late March, 1976, and we'd been looking at land for over a year. We'd dealt with many people who had wanted a lot more for a lot less. So one mild afternoon, with April in the air, the land commissioner and I donned snowshoes and circumnavigated the forty. Guiding him-self with a compass, he led me to the corners, which had been marked by blazed trees. As we shuffled along, picking our way through the brush, he pointed out the fifteen-acre lake which bordered the property on the west, a lake surrounded by government land. It would probably remain that way, he said, undeveloped and remote, with no access road. For all practical purposes, it would be ours. Beyond the lake it was six miles to the nearest lonely highway, wild country that was part of the range of a timberwolf pack. There were over a dozen lakes within five miles, the nearest neighbor was a half mile away, and the nearest tavern was four. The forty had swamp and high ground, birch and pine, aspen and fir. There was deer sign everywhere. We took it.

Land ownership has a narcotic effect. I wandered through the trees of our forty acres, bemused by three hundred years of North American history. Here was "empty" land, the stuff of countless pioneering dreams. We were on the frontier, at least in a personal sense, and we were powerful. I felt a sense of sovereignty, the rush of freedom that must have enticed settlers into the wilderness.

Land is what you need to survive, to prosper. When you control land, says History, you control your own destiny. That's why people fight over land, why Americans are jealous of their land: their land is what makes them free. This independence, nurtured by long tradition, becomes pervasive.

One spring, for instance, a friend of ours installed three marijuana plants next to the sweet corn shoots in an otherwise conventional garden. Though he attended them faithfully, fussing and coddling, they just would not take off. (The eventual harvest of THC was so low, he reported, that "you had to collapse a lung to get a buzz.")

One day in July a government pickup truck pulled into the yard and out stepped a county official. The man was an acquaintance, taking a short break from duty to say hello. He was innocently invited on a tour of the garden—it's common courtesy. You're required by local etiquette to check out a neighbor's garden, clucking approvingly over the tomatoes and corn as you would over a new car or new furniture. In this climate a good garden can be hard to come by and you must pay your respects.

The struggling marijuana was still there, half hidden by corn stalks, and was only remembered when it was too late. You couldn't just hustle this guest away from the garden—that would be rude, and suspicious. Maybe he wouldn't see it.

But as the gray-haired county official, crew-cut and nearing retirement age, surveyed the garden, noting the amazing height of the Kentucky Wonder pole beans, his eye inevitably fell on the marijuana plants. He nodded toward them and said, "Your hemp looks a little anemic. Mine is twice that size."

Relieved laughter.

"I don't use the stuff," he added. "I just grow it because they tell me I can't."

That was the traditional, backwoods-American-frontier attitude: a blend of self-reliance and devotion to principle with a touch of anarchy. It springs from a heritage of struggle that I like to think also inspired the design of our house. We were compelled by the land and the frontier tradition.

We thought that if we were going to make a life in the woods we should do it in a log cabin. We cruised through the catalogs of log-house kit manufacturers, and though the kits were attractive at first (easy and neat), we decided against a precisely tooled, twentieth-century log home. It seemed to be a contradiction. Wouldn't it be better to merge more subtly into the surrounding forest? We decided to build with rough and sundry native logs.

We first saw them the next July. There were eighty logs, stacked haphazardly in three tangled piles. They averaged about thirty-five feet in length and about fifteen inches in diameter at the butt. They were balsams, cut just two months earlier. They bore the ragged scars of a rough skidder journey through the brush, and several were caked with black mud—the rich, oozing kind you find in the worst swamps. Near their tops, the stubby, vicious remains of once-graceful limbs poked out at us. These logs were now ours; we would have to tame them.

We owed our new possessions, more or less, to a picture I had seen twenty years earlier in a children's book, a biography of Abraham Lincoln. Evenly spaced throughout the text were vivid color plates depicting various scenes from Lincoln's life. All were eye-catching, and one was unforgettable: On a winter's night, young Abe sits reading by a stone fireplace. His father is hauling an armload of firewood into the house, and through the open door one can see, in a dark blue-black sky, the bright stars of the Big Dipper. The hearth casts a warm yellow-orange glow onto Abe's book and face, and onto the magnificent log walls all around. I was entranced. The logs were solid, American, romantic. I vowed that one day I too would live in a log house, a log house that I had built myself.

My resolve was only quickened when I received a set of "Lincoln Logs" the following Christmas. The toys taught me that log construction is inherently simple. The techniques I used to build toy cabins would one day prove directly applicable to the making of our dream home in the woods. Scale would be the only difference.

But as I stood before those mountainous log piles, this matter of scale suddenly seemed critical. Not until then had I ever thought, "But can I do it?" The possibility of failure in the venture had never occurred to me. But now . . . well, look at them—entire trees!

Still, the logger had been paid ($1 per linear foot, delivered), Pam and I had just finished constructing a basement (I mixed mortar, she laid block), and we hoped to be living in our log house by winter. There was nothing to do but attack.

The first step was to unstack the logs and get them strung out along the ground on skids, where they could be peeled. A forester had told me that fresh balsam logs of that size weigh about a thousand pounds apiece, and I found no reason to quarrel with that estimate. It's fortunate that logs are round and can roll, because my tools consisted of a five-foot steel pinch bar and a peavy.

By means of simple levering, rolling, pushing, and cursing (your rudimentary machine functions), I sent the uppermost logs bouncing and crashing onto skids—spread out in rows like wieners on a grill. Deeper into the stacks, where things were tangled, the engineering became a bit more complicated. Often, one log would have to be pried up over another. Starting at the smaller, lighter end, I would use the bar to pry the log up as high as possible, and then, bracing the bar with one arm, I'd shove a board underneath the log to support it in that position. Moving farther down, I'd take another bite with the bar and repeat the procedure. Once I arrived near the middle of the log, I would have it more or less on a pivot, and I could shove it over the edge of the pile or give it a strategic roll with the peavy. It was challenging work, the kind most often performed by slaves or convicts.

Nevertheless, it turned the tide. The basic task of unpiling the logs helped me overcome the inherent hostility of objects that weigh half a ton and must be moved. I learned that I could handle those logs with hand tools, and that was good, because hand tools were all I had.

The peeling could have been worse. Balsam bark, abundant in pitch, comes off more easily than most varieties. If we'd been able to tackle the job in May, the logs would have peeled only a little less easily than bananas. By July the bark had tightened up somewhat, but even so Pam and I and a couple of friends peeled the lot in about forty hours, or a half hour per tree. For tools we used "spuds," homemade peelers fashioned from old No. 2 shovels that had been cut down into short spade-like devices and sharpened. A neighbor with a log house already under his belt had made four of these crude but effective implements, and they were passed around among a number of log builders. There were other tools and theories available, but I think these spuds were the best. You know you're in the woods when you get into an argument at the local tavern about the most efficient way to strip bark.

Through the course of peeling, and all the other functions I performed on those trunks, I acquired an intimate knowledge of "balsamness." The texture of balsam, the smell of balsam pitch, the hardness and density of balsam wood, the pattern of balsam grain, the placement of balsam limbs, the rate of balsam trunk tapering—all this is now second nature. I shall never have difficulty identifying a balsam, living or dead, and to this day a whiff of its scent induces an immediate and vivid flashback to a serene week of log peeling. It's not quite an aphrodisiac, but it's close.

Memories of the next step are not so voluptuous. Because of the thickness of the bark, all the logs had hard, protruding knots where branches had been lopped off. These had to be trimmed flush with the surface of the logs. I tried an axe but soon realized that it would take me weeks to chop off the thousands of stubs, and that in all likelihood the trees wouldn't be the only ones to lose their limbs. So I enlisted my neighbor Dick, and together we fired up our chain saws and waded into the job.

The stubs were one to three inches long, and very hard. Traces of sand clung to them, the residue of skidding, and this served to keep our chains constantly dull. Each log had to be rolled over repeatedly to get at all the knots. It was the hottest week of the summer. When we set our saws down for refueling, we had to let them cool, lest the fresh gas simply boil out of the tanks. Stripped to the waist, frequently stung by shrapnel-like chips, we sweated like pigs. One day I grazed my stomach with the near-flaming exhaust pipe of my saw. It's a curious spot for a burn scar, a rueful souvenir of the most arduous work I've ever done.

With the bark off and the last vestiges of limbs removed, the logs should have been ready for the start of construction. But we had a problem. The logger, claiming that his trucks couldn't negotiate our winding two-track road, had dropped the logs about six hundred feet from our homesite. He offered to skid them in, but that would have chewed up both the logs and the road.

So, how to transport forty tons for an eighth of a mile? I considered using my pickup in some way, but decided that I'd probably destroy it. I mused on the feasibility of pushing the logs by hand on a series of rollers, but decided that that would destroy me. Hiring someone with a loader seemed inelegant and cowardly.

I ended up borrowing a heavy-duty trailer used for hauling pipe. I could tow it with my pickup, but the edge of the trailer was three feet off the ground. Would I still have to employ a loader of some kind? No. Dick and I used inclined planes. I acquired two eighteen-foot-long bridge planks, twelve inches wide and three inches thick, and we simply rolled the logs onto the trailer and then rolled them off again at the site. It was tiring and dangerous, but also simple and cheap. As a concession to safety, I drilled holes in the planks at one-foot intervals, and we each carried a metal peg that, if necessary, we could jam into a hole behind a log to act as a brake. The Occupational Safety and Health Administration would not have been impressed.

It was the first week of August before all was ready for construction. That is not too early to be racing against the first snows. But high-quality log construction takes time, especially when you're maneuvering the logs by hand. Dick and I used a variety of methods to move and lift logs into position. Small logs, and sometimes broom handles, served as rollers under the big trunks; it was surprising how efficiently we could scoot around with half-ton loads. Lifting the logs was harder; we sometimes used a large tripod and a one-ton cable hoist. Mostly, though, we just hefted them, one end at a time, onto the walls. For heavier logs we rounded up more muscle power. Labor is cheap when it's free. (In turn, of course, I helped my helpers with their projects, gratified that I could honor a tradition that goes back at least to Seneca, who wrote, "You roll my log and I will roll yours.")

Since I'd decided to cut door and window openings as I went along, most of the logs had to be shortened, and thereby lightened, before they were notched into place, so that helped a great deal. Our basement measures twenty by thirty feet, so allowing for about eighteen inches of overhang at each end, the longest logs we had to work with were twenty-three feet and thirty-three feet. We rolled those into position using our trusty bridge planks. After the fourth course, the window level, I was able to shorten all the logs until we reached the eleventh and final course. This last row of four full-length logs is called the "cap," and it ties the structure together.

There are two basic methods for joining logs: scribing and chinking. With scribing, you notch the log for its entire length, fitting it snugly over the log beneath and leaving no space between them. Chinking requires you to notch only the ends of the logs, overlapping them at the corners as you do in scribing but leaving a gap of one or two inches along the length of the logs. The space is later filled with insulation (moss in the old days) and mortar. When most people visualize log cabins, they picture the chinked variety.

There are advantages to both methods, but I was forced to chink. Our balsam logs tapered so much that one end of a thirty-foot log could be eighteen inches in diameter and the other end just six inches. Since scribing requires you to cut a great deal of material out of a log, by the time I reached the ends of ours there would have been nothing left to work with.

But with chinking I could build faster. I found that I could produce three or four good notches per day before getting tired and sloppy; I had a total of eighty-eight to cut. It still looked as if I might make it before winter. I used a tool called a scribe to mark the notches. It's a steel caliper, or compass, designed and built by the same fellow who fabricated the bark-peeling spuds. It looks and functions like a set of tongs, but is used for measuring and marking rather than grasping. At the end of each tong there's a sharpened point for engraving the logs. I'd set a log into place, resting it on the wall where I wanted it to fit, and then with the scribe trace the contour of the log beneath onto the log to be notched. Marking this tracing with a felt-tip pen, I'd roll the log over and made a rough cut with the chain saw. Then, using a hammer and chisel and repeatedly rolling the log into position to check for a tight fit, I'd peck away at the notch until it was perfect. It was more like carving than construction.

But notch by notch, log by log, it went up. By the second week of September the walls were five logs high. Autumn was at hand, and these were golden, happy days. The sugar maples were already aflame, and the aspen and birch were just beginning to turn a luminous yellow. The evenings had a frosty edge. It seemed entirely fitting to be out in the woods erecting a log house. From my perch atop the fifth course I could see the small lake that borders our land, and beyond it the wilderness to the west. While building we had seen a black bear, several deer, and a couple of pine martens. Wolf tracks had appeared in the driveway. It was easy and irresistible to imagine that we were early settlers, and I felt in touch with that heritage as I cut the notches. I was transforming a part of the forest, entire trees, into a personal creation. We, the trees and I, exchanged the stuff of life, oxygen for carbon dioxide. Responding to the same natural cycle, our lives were intertwined under the same autumn sun. Even the cabin logs, now dead, retained a majestic composure and seemed to fall comfortably into their new role. These logs would suffer no indignities at the hands of sawyers. They were still whole trees—no longer vertical, but still beautiful and somehow vibrant.

Every log, every notch, was different, and as the walls rose higher my technique had to change. Cutting a notch while standing on a flat, stable floor was quite different from cutting a notch while balanced on a log eight or ten feet off the ground, chain saw screaming and the wind tugging at my footing. I fell once, screaming chain saw in hand, but I wasn't seriously hurt. Just deeply impressed.

Notching can't be rushed, and the log work wasn't finished

until the first week of October. On October 7 we had our first snowfall; it melted quickly, but the handwriting was on the wall. We raced to erect the second story and get a roof over it, determined to battle the elements. The first week of December found us nailing plywood to the rafters. It was 5 degrees below zero, and the roof was so icy that we had to tie ourselves to the peak and work at the ends of ropes like mountain climbers. I realized then that winter had won.

Every day through the rest of the winter I checked on our house. As the snow piled up and the northwest wind swirled it through the openings where doors and windows should have been, I felt pangs of impatience and frustrated ambition. But winter can claim only a temporary victory, and by the following July we had moved in. It was worth the wait.

For now on winter nights we watch firelight flickering along those log walls. With birch wood glowing in the stove, the logs glisten a burnished golden brown, in and out of dancing shadow. And I take pleasure in the knowledge that outside our door, in the dark northern sky, the bright stars of the Big Dipper are slowly circling Polaris.

THREE
Battleground

This nation is too civilized. That sad fact is evident when you look at almost any gardening book. Go ahead, pick one off the shelf at random. Turn to the first chapter and begin reading. Do you see the great assumption, the crucial article of faith that is invariably taken for granted?

It's hard to see at first, because most of us are long divorced from the wilderness. That's a hint. For what is assumed is the pre-existence of the garden plot itself. Oh, some books talk about soil building, organic fertilization, and such, but it's still considered a given that you have a cleared expanse of ground to begin with. Have you ever seen a discussion about cutting trees, pulling stumps, burning brush, and digging rocks—just to get to the point where you can finally start worrying about soil husbandry? Probably not.

For most of the country, that dismal chore was performed decades, or centuries, ago by generally poor, overworked, and short-lived slaves-to-the-land whom we now glamorize with the term "pioneers." It's entertaining in these soft and benign days to romanticize the deadly struggle of the pioneers, the grand adventure of "opening up the wilderness." But I suspect that if some frontier farmers were resurrected from their early graves and confronted with the corpus of popular myth, they would sardonically chuckle and then spit. I know I do.

It's not that I'm in the same league with nineteenth-century homesteaders. We cleared a measly half acre of land. Having endured that token initiation into the rigors of pioneering, I can't imagine opening up forty, eighty, or a hundred and sixty acres. It boggles the back. I pulled about fifty stumps with hand tools, and my mind is numbed to think of, say, five hundred stumps. Even if I had the benefit of an ox or a horse to aid in the extraction, it would be a daunting task. I have a lot of respect for the pioneers. Of course there are Indians alive today who still consider the whole enterprise to have been a tragic waste of time, energy, and forest, and when you drive through certain parts of the "improved" landscape—Gary, Indiana, comes to mind—it's easy to agree. And I often do, but I pulled stumps anyway. Should I have done this?

When we purchased our forty acres it was "raw" land—woods, brush, and bog—which had been logged twice since 1900 but had never been lived on. Stumps had been created, but none ever pulled. The lofty old red and white pines, the "virgin" timber, had been cut and the land left to naturally regenerate in aspen, balsam, and spruce. The biggest trees of this second generation had been logged about five years before we bought the forty, and the forest was supporting the further growth and regrowth of these species. There were no clearings as such.

We took possession of the land in the spring of 1976 and quickly decided upon a garden site. We thought it would be nice to at least get some potatoes into the ground that first season, but it didn't happen; there was just too much to be done. The road, the well, the house, all took precedence (the real pioneers would have established that garden at all costs), and it wasn't until the following spring that the spuds made it into the soil. But I worked off and on at clearing the garden site over the course of the summer, and it wasn't too bad at first.

A chain saw, in this case my only concession to the twentieth century, made felling the trees and bucking them up for firewood a relatively easy chore. There was some heavy lifting, but what the hell, it was in the job description. Slashing the brush—mostly hazel and alder with ferns, grass, and raspberry bushes—was tougher, but if I kept the edge of the brush hook sharp and swung it with authority, I made satisfactory progress. Once I had it down, I raked and tossed the brush into one huge stack, and we enjoyed a spectacular bonfire when the first snow arrived the following November. Later we spread the ashes over the cleared area to help raise the pH of the soil. It was all sweaty work, but it went quickly.

The stumps, however, were a battle. The several largest, eighteen to twenty-four inches in diameter, were like fortresses to be conquered. I had to lay a series of terrible sieges until they were broken. My weapons were the simple and timeless implements of cold steel: shovel, pick, axe, and long iron bar. It was bitter work—no quarter asked, and none given.

I launched each assault by digging in. Ramming home the blade of the shovel with my heavy lug-soled boot, I burrowed around the roots, trying to slice the smaller, stringy ones in half at the same time. They seemed to be everywhere, waiting in ambush to deflect my blade, preventing a penetration which would undermine the large, meaty roots visible from the surface. But I thrust and stomped with vigor, becoming angrier and more violent each time the shovel bounced off a small, rubbery runner. I jabbed harder, twisting and shoving, and eventually broke through to looser soil, which I scooped out and cast aside, uncovering the moist, light-colored underside of the main roots.

When the stump was surrounded, girdled by a ragged ditch, the roots exposed to cruel, dry air, I hefted my double-bit axe. Each side was honed to a wicked, glinting edge, as sharp as a butcher's knife. The three-pound head, at the end of a thirty-six-inch handle, could be brought to bear with horrible force. I raised it high over my right shoulder, then fiercely swung down, my whole torso behind the blow. There was a satisfying woody *thunk,* and the axe cut halfway through the root. I yanked it out and swung again, a little to one side of the first gash. The chips flew, scattering like shrapnel, and I struck again and again, mercilessly. The fifth blow severed the root and the axe plunged into the dirt beneath. There was a hard, grinding jolt, and I saw a spark fly. Damn! There was a rock underneath. I wrenched the axe free and examined the edge. An inch of it was flattened.

I flung it aside and grabbed the pick. With a savage looping swing I wedged the point under the root on the side of the cut away from the stump, driving it in up to the handle. Then, grasping the end of the handle, I pulled it away, leaning back with my whole 215 pounds. For a moment I strained, grunting, and then the root gave way, ripping out of the ground in a shower of dirt. I fell back on my butt.

The root had parted the soil for a length of three feet, sticking up like the tentacle of some horrid subterranean beast. I jumped up and grabbed the end, tearing it back and wresting it out of the earth. At five feet it cracked, and I twisted and yanked until it broke off.

At the stump, another blow with the pick gouged the rock out of the soil. I took the fist-sized chunk of granite and spitefully threw it as far off into the woods as I could.

Then, wielding the unblemished edge of the axe, I hacked and chopped and bashed my way through the remaining half dozen roots, hewing them off and pulling them out. That is, all of the easy ones. Each balsam also had a stubborn taproot, a large member that grew straight down from the stump and often held it securely even after all the other roots had been cut and torn away. To get at this devilish anchor I had to attack the stump itself, using the pick or the axe to rip or chop off chunks of the tough, intractable wood. Sometimes I brandished a six-pound splitting maul, sundering the stump with brute force. When I could finally see the taproot, I grabbed the five-foot bar with both hands and cocked it back like a spear. I yelled and plunged the point deep into the ground alongside the root. Then roughly, with gritted teeth and knotted biceps, I pried and pushed, back and forth, back and forth, with all my strength and anger.

Gradually the stump began to loosen, each slight movement

goading me into further jabs and lunges. In a few minutes I heard a muffled underground crack—the taproot was fractured, the stump had given up. I quickly withdrew the bar, and holding it horizontal to the ground, forced it beneath the stump, past the tortured taproot and out the other side. Bending my knees and taking several deep breaths, I jerked up on the bar as hard as I could, thrusting for the sky. With a sharp snapping-shredding sound, the stump heaved up out of the ground and rolled over on its side. Jubilant, I seized the mutilated taproot and half-dragged, half-carried the silent stump over to the brush pile. In one last ferocious gesture, I threw it vindictively onto the heap, that funeral pyre for dead wood; the only good stump was a burned stump. One down, forty-nine to go.

I sat down on the next fortress, resting. Sweat stung my eyes as I sucked on a bleeding knuckle. With my free hand I reached for the file in my back pocket—the axe needed sharpening. I looked at the wild ground that would one day be a garden. I tried to imagine the pole beans and the lush sugar snap peas, the sweet corn waving in the August sun. It didn't work. All I saw was more stumps and the shattered remains of hazel brush. I lifted my eyes and there was the forest, dense and alive with trees I wouldn't touch. I could see a blue jay flitting through the branches. Was I doing a good thing? After three centuries of expansion, did more land need to be "opened up"? Was I improving the land? I had my doubts.

It was like the power line right-of-way we helped a friend to clear. Unless your homesite is hopelessly remote, the REA (Rural Electrification Administration) will supply electricity to you, but you are responsible for opening a way through the woods. It's rigorous, depressing work.

We began in January. The strip was to be thirty feet wide and two miles long. There were hundreds of trees to be killed, acres of brush to be slaughtered. For six months, whenever we had the time, we hacked and sawed and burned. It was a rite of brutalization. It is difficult to cultivate a respect for living plants when you cut down and buck up a couple dozen trees at a crack. With chain saws roaring and smoking, we industriously produced stumps, brush piles, and firewood.

The Ojibway who originally occupied this land would no doubt have been horrified. It is reported that the Ojibway seldom took down a living tree, because they believed that a tree could feel pain; their medicine men are said to have heard trees wailing under the axe. Many other primitive tribes around the world have been similarly circumspect in their treatment of green trees. The Basoga of central Africa, for instance, sacrificed animals to each tree they were about to fell.

Needless to say, such amenities would have cramped our style. Our education and cultural heritage had somehow neglected to deal with trees as anything more romantic or sentient than raw materials or bothersome obstacles (in spite of Joyce Kilmer). We made no apologies to the doomed trunks. Except one.

It was a majestic, perfectly formed spruce—three feet in diameter at the butt and about sixty-five feet high. Standing near the road on a gentle rise, it was the ruler of all it surveyed, a great Houdini of a tree that, almost alone among its peers, had escaped the ravages of men and their saws, of lightning, of fire, of disease, and of insects. Truly it was a graceful tree, with no defects to mar the perfect arcs of its healthy boughs or the straightness of its massive trunk. It had only one flaw—and that a tragic one. It stood in our path.

To our credit, we really didn't want to kill that tree. We were weary of sawdust and smoke, and we wanted no part in the demise of this awesome living thing. But we hadn't cut and slashed a distance of two miles for nothing, and the big spruce was clearly in the way. It had to come down.

To lend some dignity to the tree's end, I went down to the hardware store and bought a brand-new double-bit axe. Such a pristine giant could not be finished off with a mean and vulgar chain saw. We assembled food, beer, and friends for an event we billed The Final Tree Party. The beer was a good idea; I needed about three before I could bring myself to start the fateful undercut. About a dozen spectators gathered around the base of the spruce as I fired up my saw. It sounded a little tinny. I winced as the chain chewed away the first layer of rough bark and bit into the wood. All the veterans of our recent work took turns at the saw. There is safety in numbers, and guilt, like many other things, is better shared.

With the first cut finished, and with a triangular wedge from the living tree lying in the sawdust, we lined up on the unmarred side for our turns with the virgin axe. Each ringing blow was a death knell for the old spruce, which was giving up its life in chips and chunks of aromatic heartwood. It did not go gently. Any one of the last twenty-five or thirty whacks should have brought it down. Again and again, what we thought would surely be the coup de grace had no visible effect. Suspense began to build, but we refused to rekindle the chain saw.

Finally the distant top began to list. We hurriedly backed off. In agonizingly slow motion, the huge tree leaned past the critical point and whispered to the ground, the fall cushioned by its boughs. The whole tree bounced a little, and then the quivering branches fell still. The butt was ten feet off the ground. The loudest noise had been a short, sharp crack as the trunk separated from the stump. We heard no wailing.

We left a great gap in the sky, a hole which will take seventy years to refill. Instead of spruce boughs, the birds have wires to perch on. A dubious achievement.

FOUR
A Gift of Ice

A house rises slowly. A home, hand built and stained with the sweat (and a little of the blood) of those who will live in it, even slower. We had plenty of time to wander down to the lake and watch for loons and beaver.

We discovered there were a number of dead aspens lying near the edge of the muskeg, the broken residue of a vicious storm which had torn through the stand a few years before. In my "spare" time I bucked them up into four-foot lengths and constructed a crude corduroy path across fifty feet of spongy bog to the edge of the open water.

I portaged our canoe down there and left it, and in the evenings we often paddle out to watch the sun set into the forest. It's a quiet, contemplative time, unless an otter happens to be visiting.

As near as I've been able to determine, otters, as a species, are greatly offended by aluminum canoes. A normally playful lot, almost frivolous as mammals go, otters will turn livid at the approach of an aluminum canoe. At least they have every time I've been around in one.

A large female with two kits once surfaced a mere ten feet from our canoe, hissing and spitting. She actually made two short, lunging charges in our direction, her sinuous body undulating with menace, like a furry serpent. For a moment I wished I had Jimmy Carter and his oar in there with us; I thought we were going to do battle.

But such a ruckus is an exception on "our" lake. Being small, it's often placid; the chief ripples are made by the lips of feeding perch or the nose of a watering deer.

I spend a lot of time watching the lake. The variations of sunlight, weather, and seasons, along with the natural flexibility of water, ensure that you rarely see it exactly the same way twice. But there is a general pattern, a process of design, and we noted what I considered to be the best part of it through the course of our first seasons on the land.

It began in late September, in those waning golden weeks when cool northern air stalks the weary summer at dusk. As the sun set behind a stand of black spruce across the lake, tendrils of white mist began to form along the edges of the muskeg and waft gently over the lake. Late-September air met early-August water, and though the sun blazed warm the next morning, the lake had begun to freeze. There would be no ice crystals for another month or so, but the inevitable had begun.

By mid-October, fog shrouded the lake on frosty mornings. Stored sunshine of summer escaped into the autumn sky, dissipating into water-vapor clouds as morning by morning, degree by degree, the seasonal ice age approached.

One night in the first week of November, the mercury dipped into the teens. By morning a rim of ice handcuffed the water. The next night the temperature eased below zero, and the liquid lake was entombed beneath a solid sheet of ice a quarter inch thick. No wind came the next day to break it up. The open water was gone.

Day by day, an unseasonable cold snap nurtured the young ice. November sunlight glared off the sheet each afternoon, but there was no conviction in it. The sun's only remaining gift was its light. The short, weak days were but foils for the long arctic nights.

It seems that every year, just before the heavy snows finally bury all traces of autumn, a handful of fair days briefly grace the land. That year was no exception. The three inches of snow that had fallen before Thanksgiving melted away, leaving newly white rabbits defenseless and the frozen lake covered with a thin film of water. Then a wondrous thing followed. The normally rough, bumpy ice was leveled and smoothed just in time for colder nights to refreeze it, leaving a near-perfect, glass-like surface—a fifteen-acre skating rink. It was a hard sheet of ice, six inches thick and so clear that you could see fish swimming below. For days the lake remained free of snow, and daylight temperatures hovered in the 30s.

It was a rare gift. What a joy to lace up skates and cruise, gliding past trees and muskeg as if on a summer canoe ride. What a thrill to tear straight across the ice at full speed and to stop from exhaustion, not because you'd run out of ice. What could compare to darting in and out along the frozen shoreline, watching ice-encased lily pads flashing by beneath your feet? An entire lake surrounded by forest; a solitary skater, master of it all.

I twirled and spun on a field of glass, my skate blades flashing and cutting, my face burning from the cold and the exhilaration. Such moments ache with pleasure. They cry out in sheer delighted defiance of the limits of time and space. I grinned and laughed and shouted. The frozen lake was the universe, and I was immortal.

I skated until dark, happy and free. The waxing quarter moon was winter-bright as I unlaced my skates. I was almost surprised that the blades weren't hot to the touch. I slipped on my boots and stood, a gesture of finality that I expected would end the magic of that day. But it was not to be. Standing quietly on the ice, a few feet from shore, I heard a low, muffled moan—a full but dim resonance, like a grouse drumming, or like a night wind in the eaves. At first I thought it was the echo of a distant explosion. Then I felt a vibration beneath my feet. It was the ice.

Again and again, the ice sheet groaned. The rumble echoed off the trees, punctuated now and then by a sharp crack. As my ears adjusted I heard other, distant groanings—the expanding ice of nearby lakes. In deep winter the snow muffles the eerie music of the ice, but on this night all the lakes were cold and bare. I was listening to a symphony of freezing lakes, massive sheets of ice releasing the stress of their growth in heaving cracks that wailed softly in birth. It transfixed me with its simple, awesome power. Nothing that any man could ever do would change the tune of the ice.

It began in September with wisps of evening mist. It ended with tons of cold, hard ice grumbling in the early winter moonlight. It was difficult to believe that I'd ever see open water again. Or care to.

But there's another way to see the ice, a different means for measuring its power. And on "our" lake I've experienced that as well.

It was another November, another lustrous sheet of ice, and I gratefully dusted off my skates for the season. But in a few minutes, disaster.

I instantly knew I was seriously hurt. Sometimes the shock and swiftness of an injury can disguise its severity, but not this time. There was shock and it happened fast, but I knew my left arm was useless. I was trying to make it work and it wouldn't. It crossed my mind that with only one good arm I might die. With my skates on.

We'd been skating down the lake, enthralled by the clear, smooth ice. It was new, two inches thick, transparent as glass. We could spot an occasional fish darting away beneath our blades. My buddy Sooch was equipped with a cassette player and headphones, skating and jumping to the rhythms of Bruce Springsteen. I couldn't hear the music, but I could see the "vibes" reflected in Sooch's jerky rock-and-roll figure eights. He was definitely tuned in.

Liberated by flying skates, I sprinted down the shoreline ahead of Sooch, trying to go as fast as possible, seeing how fleet the ice could make me.

And then it happened. What else to say about a sprung trap? I was streaking along, high and free, and then I was in the water, stopped cold and thrashing in agony up to my neck. The ice, with no warning on the surface, no cracks or puddles, had given way. My skates plunged through and the impetus of my forward motion flung my torso onto the hard, frozen shore. My left arm, outstretched in a pumping swing, took the brunt of the blow. With all my weight behind it, the arm was violently twisted back behind my head—much farther than it was designed to go. The bone of my upper arm was ripped out of the shoulder socket, and it felt like an explosion in the tissues.

Stunned by pain and surprise, I slid off the shore and into the frigid water. It lapped at my chin and I began to struggle. I clutched at icy tufts of grass on the bank, trying to gain a purchase. The left arm felt disembodied, like fumbling with some clumsy, inefficient remote control. The fingers worked, but when I used them to reach for the grass, a stab of fierce, savage pain stormed the length of the arm and focused in the shoulder, throbbing. It forced a cry from my constricted throat. I grabbed a clump of grass with my right hand, and kicking with soggy, leaden skates, I lunged out of the water to my waist.

But the frosty blades of grass slipped through my glove and I slid back into the water up to my chest. Where was Sooch? I grabbed another handful of grass and heaved up again. This time I bashed a knee up through the ice and got it partway onto land. Levering and lurching like a frantic crab, I managed to slither out of the hole in the ice and onto the shore.

I was soaked to the skin and could feel the wetness, but I didn't feel cold. I knew I should be freezing, but that sensation was apparently being shunted aside in the neural circuits. All I could feel was the lashing, knifing pain in my left arm.

I rolled onto my back and writhed a little bit before sitting up, and that's when Sooch, still plugged into his electronics, finally saw me "flopping around like a crappie." He could tell something was wrong, he said later, by the funny, twisted shape of my mouth. He couldn't hear anything but Springsteen, but my mouth looked to him as if it was uttering wretched and beastly sounds. Actually, I was bearing the pain in relative silence, treating myself to an intermittent grunt or epithet. My anger had good cause: one of the first items which came to mind once I was out of the lake was the truly frightening fact that I was presently without medical insurance. Nothing will put a damper on a serious accident faster than the prospect of doctor's bills.

As Sooch skated up to peer at me and the hole I'd made in our rink, I pointed at my left arm and explained, "Arm!" He noticed a strange bulge in the sleeve of my jacket. He nodded and cocked an eyebrow. "You aren't going to pass out or something silly like that, are you?"

I grunted that no, I was sure I could skate away from this one.

"Good," he replied. "I could probably slide your carcass across the ice, but skidding you out of the woods would be rough, especially on my skates."

Ouch. It would be a shame to dull a skate blade.

We glided back across the lake to where we'd left our boots, Sooch circling his hunched-over, listing-to-port companion, waiting to break the inevitable fall. But I made it, inspired by the notion that if I fell on that arm again, I no doubt would pass out.

We'd lugged a kitchen chair down to the lake so we could don our skates like gentlemen, and when we reached the shore I eased down onto it, shattering the film of ice that covered my pants. Sooch, businesslike and efficient, obviously enjoying the opportunity to aid a wounded creature, quickly unlaced my skates and snuggled me into my boots. Then, looking like a cross between Quasimodo and a muskrat, I stumbled up the forest path to the house and presented this sorry aspect to Pam.

"We've got to go to the hospital," I greeted her, standing morosely in the puddle of cold water that formed on the floor as soon as I entered the house. If it hadn't been for the word "hospital," she probably would have laughed. It was obvious what had happened, and my semiannual skating-swimming routine had already become a minor local legend. Just a couple of years before I had tried to leap a narrow stretch of open water on Little Sturgeon Lake, and didn't make it. I tend to become exuberant on skates, overconfident of my abilities, intoxicated by fun. The year before that I'd . . . Well, it really is too tiresome. ("Hey, Leschak, how's the water this winter?")

Pam also noted the strange bulge in my sleeve, and with much snorting, yelping, and exclaiming, she and Sooch and I managed to wriggle me out of the soaking jacket.

"Dislocated shoulder," Sooch announced. "We just put a foot in your armpit and give her a yank."

Sure. "To the hospital," I repeated.

Even as I spoke the words I knew it was a matter easier said than done. The thing about living twenty miles from town is that you're twenty miles from town. I've yet to see a billboard advertising The Backwoods Medical Center (and Taxidermy).

The ride into town was worse than I expected. Every bump and crack in the road sent a jolt through my arm, and the rest of the time it stung and throbbed. Pam attempted to strike a balance between speed and comfort, and I tried for stoicism, but we both missed the mark.

As the decade-long ride grew to a close and we approached the town limits, Pam suggested we try the clinic rather than the hospital. The gist of her argument was that since I was conscious and not bleeding, the hospital would send me over there anyway. I disagreed, firmly convinced I was an emergency case and belonged in an honest-to-goodness emergency room. She remained skeptical but headed for the hospital, not wishing to argue with the contorted figure who was spitting sharp words from between gritted teeth and pulling at its hair with white and sweaty fingers.

But sure enough, no sooner was I installed on one of those adjustable multipurpose torture-chamber examining tables than the nurse on duty returned and said it "would be better" if we took my troubles over to the clinic. As I shuffled out the door into the cold, still in my wet clothes and bent over at the waist, she asked me if it hurt. I admitted that it did. She offered a wheelchair. No, shuffling was okay.

After a two-year drive to the clinic, I was fixed up with another high-tech examining table and invited to sit down, but I opted to just lean against it. Sitting down implied standing up again, and my cockeyed bone found that move unacceptable.

After several minutes of deep meditation upon the texture and meaning of agony, the medical establishment did me a kindness. A nurse helped me fumble with my belt buckle and drop my pants, and then slipped me a hypo of Demerol to "aid relaxation." That's what I was there for.

After shooting up, the wheelchair was apparently mandatory, the price to be paid for good drugs, and I was trundled off to X-ray. I understood the wisdom of reconnaissance in the arm and shoulder, the need to scout around for possible fractures, but the intelligence was dearly gained. The X-ray technician insisted upon high-quality images with good composition, and I had to twist, or was made to twist, my arm into attitudes that overrode the Demerol. I discovered the height of black humor: prod and bend an injured man until the pain has set him to trembling, and then duck behind a camera and order him to sit still.

When my photo opportunity was over, I spurned the wheelchair and hobbled back to the examining table. I meditated for several more minutes and then two nurses entered the room. They told me the doctor was on his way and he wanted me lying on my stomach on the table with my injured arm hanging down over the side. Hmm. Why not just juggle three machetes while walking a tightrope?

But we tried it. With the nurses awkwardly shoving on my thighs and butt, and me struggling ineffectually with my good arm, I tried to mount the examining table. If we had the scene on film, we could probably find some kinky market for it. After several spasms of pain, we had me flopped across the table, sideways, my left arm dangling free and at the limit of abuse. I was just suggesting we try something else when I felt the bone slip back into its socket. The pain vanished. I know how the man felt when Jesus told him to get up and walk. Just like that, I was healed. I stood up smiling.

"Hey, I could have done this at home," I said.

One of the nurses emitted a polite snicker. "You've got a hypo full of Demerol in your medicine cabinet?" Good point.

The doctor strode in and said he was happy to see the shoulder had eased back together. Otherwise he'd have had to put a foot in my armpit and give her a yank. Scout's honor—he learned it in medical school.

In any case, I finally started to shiver. The pain was gone and I could be cold now. They wrapped me in a sling and a blanket, and Pam drove me home. The bill came to $93.50. In this day and age, that's pretty cheap entertainment.

Of course, in the backwoods, cheap is just about the only kind of entertainment there is. But of all the low-priced diversions available, surely the least expensive is volunteer labor. Being relatively remote and therefore uncoddled by government, we've enjoyed a lot of that over the years.

For example, when Side Lake decided to build a hockey rink— an almost inevitable decision in this part of the world—we realized that we would have to rely totally on Ronald Reagan's vision of a spontaneously helpful America full of volunteers aching to take up the slack caused by his budget cuts. There may have been a time in the decadent past when we could have received government funding for such a project (perhaps under the auspices of the Head Start program, whereby we would train four-year-olds for future glory in the National Hockey League). But in our neoconservative fervor, we didn't even try for it.

With seed money graciously donated by a pillar of Side Lake's private sector, about thirty volunteers set to work in November— laboring, naturally enough, under the self-appointed foremanship of the man with the bucks. (How neatly these heady management questions work themselves out in a small-scale operation.) With the snows due any day, we rink rats (a communal term of endearment) built the boards at a feverish pace. It must have been an inspiring sight to any passing Republican, though my informal survey revealed that most of the workers were lukewarm Democrats, unwitting socialists, or closet anarchists. I recognized the beauty of Mr. Reagan's volunteering scheme when I stopped hammering and looked around. These folks had time to build a hockey rink because most of them were laid off, unemployed, on strike, or indigenous derelicts. They had nothing better to do than build a hockey rink. Take heart, America: idle hands are being put to work.

Part of the charm of a community project is that it gives everyone an opportunity to show his neighbors what he can do, or what his fantasies tell him he can do. One would-be engineer showed up with a transit to help us level the ground between the boards. He looked quite official as he peered through the instrument, making significant hand signals and delicately adjusting the focusing knob. The effect was ruined, sadly, by his level rod—a scrap of one-by-four lumber with lines and numbers in a felt-tip scrawl. Our final grade was apparently not critical. The key phrase here was "close enough."

Another fellow, who runs a restaurant in real life, arrived astride an ancient tractor (Eighteenth Dynasty, I believe) to spend a few hours smoothing out rough spots. He obviously relished the chance to imagine himself in the more romantic role of heavy-equipment operator.

With the boards securely in place, the ground reasonably level, and the temperature below freezing (we northerners pride ourselves on the knowledge that this is a critical consideration in the formation of ice), the local volunteer fire department began to flood the rink. We do not have the luxury of fire hydrants out here in the country; such opulence is reserved for recognized centers of civilization, and in northern Minnesota there are none nearby. (In fairness, I should mention that I did hear a case built for Duluth one night at the bar.) We rink rats had to string seven hundred feet of fire hose down to the river and employ a portable pump to deliver the necessary water. "Portable" is a quaint term for a rig that could simultaneously herniate four grown men.

If you've never flooded an ice rink, the task no doubt seems simple. You just pour water on the ground and let it freeze, right? Horrors—unless, of course, what you want is the sort of ice that causes tractor-trailers to jackknife on the freeway. What we were after is that finely crafted crystalline surface on which the likes of Wayne Gretzky and Dorothy Hamill amaze the masses. That kind of ice is not simply frozen water. It is pampered, layered, and above all, textured frozen water. Our rink achieved this blissful state only after trial, error, anguish, and the application of several thousand gallons of raw material.

We had received some good advice about ice at the start, but— as often happens with volunteers, smug in their dedication and full of their own ideas—we ignored it in favor of extra work. Volunteers have a strong instinct to keep busy (which tends to make me a little nervous about the volunteer army). In our case, we now have a hard-core cadre of icemakers who will devote themselves to their newfound calling until death or the spring thaw, whichever comes first. That the two are likely to run neck-and-neck became clear when we had our first "adult" hockey game.

To understand northern Minnesota's adult-hockey leagues, it helps to remember that hockey is the region's unofficial religion, the stuff that dreams are made of. If you happen to be a hockey star in high school, you can play for any college in the nation. You have a crack at the Olympic team, and maybe even the pros. Even such a dubious goal as public office is not out of reach. Hockey worked for ex-governor Wendy Anderson—and what else could have?

Local adult leagues are full of players who did not make the big time. In many cases this shortcoming has wrought permanent psychological damage. Imagine a Texan who has reached the age of majority without ever owning a pickup truck, and you begin to grasp the magnitude of the injury. These frustrated hockey stars carry a personal passion to the game that makes it something far more than recreation. As they hurtle down the ice—dodging, darting, "deeking"—they are not Mr. Average Guy out for a little exercise; they are fearsome crusaders avenging adolescent fantasies that suffered but never quite died.

Our first game—our first game with both a timekeeper and a modest amount of official decorum—was a close one. We lost 8–7 to the Bear River boys, even though the partisan timekeeper gave us two extra minutes to try for a tie. The goalies made the difference. The Bear River goalie was the quintessential frustrated star. He tended goal as if he were in Madison Square Garden before thousands of rabid fans, not in Side Lake, Minnesota, in front of a couple dozen friends and relatives. He played as if in search of an inexpensive vasectomy or lobotomy (though it seemed entirely possible that a lobotomy would be redundant). Our goalie, on the other hand, had a measure of respect for his own body—no doubt a healthy and healthful characteristic in the long run, but scarcely an ideal trait for a goalie.

Generally, the game was played with reckless abandon. Several of the Side Lakers had not played hockey in years; they had already resigned themselves to normal adult life and, eventually, death. But souls were reawakened that night, and faces glowed with the exhilaration of controlled mayhem. Beyond the customary bruises, I'm happy to report, no one was injured. But it's only a matter of time. The reigning philosophy seems to be that a hockey rink is not a hockey rink until there is a little blood on the ice. A little blood on the ice is a demonstration of sincerity, a kind of consecration.

The lure of the newly built rink was strong, especially for people who had no business being there. One retired gentleman stumbled drunkenly onto the ice, without skates, and proceeded to act as goalie—or rather, target—for some of the younger players. For more than an hour he lurched around in front of the net as pucks whizzed by (they almost all whizzed by) at various deadly altitudes and velocities. As he struggled off the ice, he said, "Hell, if I woulda been sober, I coulda done a lot better out there."

"Jim," came the reply, "if you'd been sober, you wouldn't have been out there at all."

How true. What, for that matter, were any of us doing out there? We were voluntarily drenching ourselves with water in subzero cold, shoveling tons of snow off the ice every week, playing hockey with a confidence that should have been long tempered by reality. It is a startling phenomenon. Even during the drudgery of snow removal, worker morale was high. I wonder if the Japanese might be interested in this? Certainly Mr. Reagan should be. I can see the political slogan now: "A rink in every town, and rats on every rink." In place of the dismal "President," Reagan could call himself "Lord of the Rinks."

That way, instead of the President's economic advisors hogging the fun, we could all indulge in a little fantasy.

# IVE
Fire!

The truth is, we don't often need the President in Side Lake. Oh, it's nice to know that he's off in distant and ethereal Washington, hand on the tiller of the executive branch, taking credit or blame for the United States as a whole, but we don't deal much with the Feds, at least not directly. (Of course most everyone is on the mailing list of the IRS.)

We have township government in Side Lake, a political entity that many modern Americans associate with the eighteenth century, or with dinosaurs. We're not the incarnation of Thomas Jefferson's vision of virtuous yeoman farmers governing themselves (none of us are farmers), but we're close. The last census showed 156 year-round households scattered over thirty-six square miles of forest, so we're small enough for effective government to remain personal and human.

The township Board of Supervisors meets in an old one-room schoolhouse. The kids have long since been bussed to town, but the school paraphernalia is still there, providing an apt setting for the machinations of local American government. The hardwood-rimmed blackboards (that are really black) often bear the simple budgetary figures which everyone understands. You can actually perform simple arithmetic on our treasurer's numbers, and it works.

I guess that's one reason George Washington looks so satisfied. His portrait, the one which appears to show a cloud rising up to his shoulders, hangs above the blackboard. It's the picture that hung in almost every one of my classrooms from kindergarten through twelfth grade. It has a religious aura about it—the Great White Father. Naturally Old Glory is in the corner, and sometimes I feel the urge to rise and recite the Pledge of Allegiance. It would sound just right in that room.

The town board grapples with the basics: roads, fire protection, property lines. Since we built the rink and a ball field, they also dabble in recreation. Most of the meetings are boring, and that's comforting. It's the way government should be.

That's not to say we don't chuckle now and then. At a recent meeting one of the hot topics was the streetlight (we have a half dozen at some otherwise empty intersections) south of the fire tower. It had been shot out twice in the space of a few months, and after being repaired only a few weeks before, it was out yet again. There are some folks who believe that if you want light at night, you should move to town. Nights are for stars and dark bedrooms.

The town clerk noted the light was out, but she didn't check to see if it was shot out. She speculated that perhaps it merely burned out, though it didn't seem likely since it was so recently repaired.

Jerry, one of the supervisors: "Probably isn't burned out. I put a light like that one in my yard back in seventy-nine, and it's still burning."

Dick, another supervisor: "Hell, Jerry, you're just a lousy shot."

Streetlights aren't to be taken too seriously.

Not so with the volunteer fire department. I served time as the fire chief, and it scared me half to death. Side Lake is small and unknown, almost lost in the woods. We don't shake the earth (or even the county), but when you respond to a fire call you have precisely the same responsibility as a fire fighter in New York City—human life.

I lost sleep thinking about fires, especially about what could happen if one of our few public places burned, like Pine Beach Resort. A lot of people could be endangered by such a blaze. I hoped I wouldn't be the chief when and if that happened; I wouldn't want to shoulder that burden. My hope was in vain.

The alarm came through at 10:30 P.M. We were just settling into bed when the pager-receiver made a short, sharp squawk and the voice of the dispatcher at the sheriff's department filled the house. "Sheriff's office calling the Town of French Fire Department. There is a fire reported at Pine Beach Resort."

The voice was calm, almost flat, as always, but I felt the bottom of my stomach fall away. Pine Beach Resort was one of the largest structures in our jurisdiction, and unlike many of the seasonal homes in this rural lakeside community, it was almost certain to be occupied.

As I rushed to get dressed, Pam, who is also a fire fighter, phoned three others in the department. Being an entirely volunteer outfit in a sparsely populated area, our budget is small. We can't afford pagers for all twenty-five members. Each fire fighter who has one of the department's ten pagers must alert two or three who don't. Even so, there is no way to determine how many people will show up at a fire until you actually arrive on the scene. This makes for nerve-wracking drives down dark backwoods roads. What if we're the only ones who respond? What if everyone else is at work, sick, on vacation, away from the phone, or dealing with some emergency of their own? Our only consolation is that so far it's never happened. Folks who are impossible to reach with a dinner invitation materialize almost instantly for a fire.

A couple of years ago, a sauna fire routed us out of bed at 2 A.M. on a subzero February night. The structure was a half mile from the nearest plowed road, so neither our fire trucks nor any other vehicles could even get close. Nevertheless, within fifteen minutes nine fire fighters had arrived and a portable pump was being towed in behind a snowmobile. Pam and I, seeing the flames from the road near the shore of the lake, ran across the ice. There was no charged hose immediately available, so people shoveled snow against the side of the nearby house to cool it down and prevent it from catching fire as well. The owner was amazed by the number of people running around his yard at that ungodly hour.

I took it as a positive omen that on this January night, when a 40-below temperature wouldn't have been at all unusual, Mother Nature at least was cooperating. It's always depressing to see water freeze even as it leaves the hose. The weather was far from balmy, but the thermometer told us that it was above zero. When I was elected fire chief, one of my campaign promises was "No more fires after midnight or in subzero weather." So far so good, but Pam and I both gasped as we crossed the bridge near Little Sturgeon Lake. Across the ice off to the east, at the tops of distant pines, an ominous orange glow colored the sky.

It's not unusual for fire fighters who live in the wilderness to arrive at the scene only to find the structure already burned to the slab. Because most buildings are surrounded by forest, smoke and flame are often not visible to neighbors. Our chief function is therefore to save outbuildings, the house "next door," and the forest itself. We have a rueful little motto: We've never lost a lot. "Lot," as in plot of ground. (I did hear a tale from another fire department about a house that burned near a peat bog; the peat was ignited and the owner lost his lot as well as his house.)

After a three-mile drive, we pulled into the parking area at Pine Beach. Two fire trucks had just arrived. Much to my joy, several fire fighters were there too, throwing on protective gear and dragging hoses out of the trucks. (Eventually, twenty of our twenty-five members would show up.) Pulling on a helmet, coat, and boots, I began to assess the damage.

Pine Beach was a big building, housing a restaurant, bar, dance floor, and guest rooms. It had been the scene of community social events since it was built in the 1930s. This was not just another fire call, this was a disaster—the blaze we all had feared as we trained. I'd been chief for less than five months. I had dreaded each alarm, expecting it to be the Big One. Finally it had come.

A tongue of smoke-streaked flame had just broken through the roof—a very bad sign, but not as disturbing as the news that two men were inside, in the second-story apartments. There are few things in the world more dangerous than entering a burning building, but someone had to go after those men. The department has only two Scott Air-Paks, self-contained breathing apparatus similar to scuba gear. I called out to Andy, one of our most experienced members, a former commercial pilot, a man with a cool head; and to Gene, an EMT (emergency medical technician). We have always been a nonauthoritarian group—I asked them, politely but firmly, if they would don the Air-Paks and go inside.

Both responded with a look that combined resistance, acquiescence, and fear. The look said, "Why *me?*" and "Who the hell do you think *you* are?" and "Of course I'll go!" Out loud they said nothing. They grabbed the cases containing the Air-Paks.

By this time the intense heat had melted the snow off the roof, and despite the cold weather everyone within thirty feet of the building was sweating. Gray-black smoke billowed out from every crack. Visibility inside would be zero, and it was impossible to tell if the second-story floor would support two men. Gene and Andy would have to make their way on all fours, praying for courage and luck. I was scared, but this fire was why we'd joined the fire department. We'd volunteered to save property, but even more important, to save lives if it came to that. This is what brings a group of virtual strangers, some of them reclusive by nature, together on cold winter nights. Aside from living in the same area, we have little in common. We're not a social club (though we put on a mean annual picnic), but we know what to expect from each other in a crisis, and that knowledge forms a bond.

Occasionally the bond is strong enough even to endure a noncrisis. For example, a few years ago, when some citizens of Side Lake decided to organize a civic association to promote and implement local improvement projects, they turned to the fire department for help. We were the only organized body in the community with a long tradition of service and a certain esprit de corps. We supplied direction and labor for the original fundraiser in behalf of the new association and, I like to think, some inspiration as well.

While Andy and Gene were preparing to enter the building, the rest of us laid out over a thousand feet of hose and hauled two portable pumps onto the frozen lake. Without fire hydrants, and with trucks able to hold only a token two thousand gallons, we must rely upon lakes and rivers for the bulk of our water. Our man out there on the ice drill gives a whole new meaning to the phrase "ace in the hole." The ice was about eighteen inches thick, and the instant the drill punched through and dark water broke to the surface, suction lines were shoved into the holes and the pumps started heaving. We ran two inch-and-a-half hoses off each pump. Four men clutching the nozzles staggered as the first water rushed through the lines.

The nozzlemen approached the building slowly, trying to judge how far out a blazing wall would reach if it should fall. They headed for the hot spots and turned their hoses on the building. It was a discouraging sight. Like an incandescent version of a black hole, the inferno seemed to swallow up the icy water and dispatch it to oblivion.

Andy and Gene were now ready, moving grimly toward the front of the flaming resort. Their face masks reflected the orange glow from the roof above. Grasping a charged hose which would double as a lifeline, they approached the door that served the upstairs apartments. I went ahead of them to open it, but the knob wouldn't budge. I hauled back and gave it a good kick, and the door flew open upon a stairway engulfed in flames. Even as we watched, a blackened and fiery joist fell onto the stairs. It was clear that entry would be suicidal. We turned on the hose and backed away. Anyone inside was dead. That meant a grisly body search in the morning, and yet I was relieved. Our men were safe.

A few minutes later an explosion shook what remained of Pine Beach Resort. Everyone automatically covered their faces and ducked as sparks shot up out of the flames now devouring the building, spraying the sky with twisting red patterns created by the violent convection currents. We all backed off, waiting for a second blast, but it never came.

Now our task was to contain the fire, to protect the nearby cabins. It would take all night. I found a telephone and reported the blaze to the local fire marshall, informing him that I feared casualties. He said he would come out at dawn.

Pam, meanwhile, was on the phone trying to locate the couple who owned Pine Beach. We'd heard they were in town for the evening, but we failed to track them down. By the time they returned to the resort, shortly after midnight, the huge structure had collapsed. Steel support girders were twisted into outlandish shapes. All that remained of the resort was a large stone fireplace and chimney.

The owners' reaction was painful to watch. A horrified exclamation, a scream of anguish, a collapse into the arms of friends and relatives. But we were relieved to learn that one of the men we feared lost in the blaze had returned with the owners. And he assured us that the other man, too, was safe—the building had been empty after all. That made the night, and the prospect of the morning, a lot less dreary.

As the night wore on, the owners became at least a little reconciled to the devastating spectacle before them, and they began to exhibit behavior I've seen time and again, but still find surprising. In the midst of their loss, when you'd expect them to be too dejected to respond, they can't stop heaping affection on the fire fighters. Here is a person's house, business, or whatever, more than likely gutted or lying in smoking ruins, and there they are, thanking, congratulating, and praising us. In most cases we haven't even saved the place, and still people laud our efforts and often promise monetary donations to the department— promises that are invariably kept. I'm always a bit embarrassed when this happens, especially if the structure was a total loss. You wish you could have done more, and sometimes blame yourself for variables of time and distance that were beyond your control. To the owners, though, you appear as angels of mercy. You responded to their call for help, and they can see that you tried your best. They are deeply moved that fellow members of their community came running through the winter night or pouring rain, setting aside their own concerns or leaving a warm bed, and put their health and safety on the line. It injects a note of hope and camaraderie into an otherwise dismal situation and goes a long way toward helping people through the crisis of personal loss.

By 3 A.M. the fire had died down to a few smoldering pockets. The danger to adjacent property was over, and I formed a skeleton crew of myself and three others to man the hoses until dawn. The rest returned to their beds. As I played the hose over blackened, unrecognizable shapes, picking my way through the wreckage at the edge of the ruins, I was struck by the realization of what had been lost. Throughout the night I had been a fire fighter doing his job; now I was a mourner, overwhelmed with fond memories of Pine Beach Resort. How many times had we danced there, laughing and carousing until closing? How many wedding vows had we celebrated? How many new years?

Then I remembered the wood carvings. At the time the place was built, a long since forgotten craftsman had created a series of six monumental silhouette carvings depicting familiar local scenes and activities. I'd admired them for thirty years, recalling how they'd impressed me as a child. They were community heirlooms, meant to be there always, generation after generation, to remind you of home. Now they were gone, irreplaceable.

Then I looked over at my three tired and dirty companions, volunteers who had stayed to see this fire through to the end, and I felt comforted. A shared disaster isn't quite so much of a disaster. The community might even be stronger for the loss.

Six

Beasts of Burden

The best thing about log walls is the way they feel. Not to your fingertips (though it is nice to run a hand along the smooth, tung-oiled trunks); it's the way they feel in your mind. Like this:

I'm nestled into an old, familiar rocker, my feet aimed at the wood stove. Next to the stove lies an elderly, overweight golden retriever, evenly breathing in deep sleep. The cat is a soft, warm bundle in my lap, her tail over her eyes. A good book is cradled in my hands; I may read it. Pam is comfortable on the couch, tying flies and dreaming of open water. We know that outside snow is falling, crowding onto the roof for a prolonged stay.

My eyes wander from the book to the logs. Their stalwart passivity is highlighted by the dimness. They aren't going anywhere. These solid trees form a bastion of security, and I can pick out individuals, like old pals.

There, at the bottom, is the first log we laid. It's a half log, neatly ripped in two so its flat side fits snugly against the plywood subfloor. It's called a starter log, and its other half is at the opposite end of the house. The first two full logs, round and massive, were notched into these halves.

Using a borrowed boat trailer, I had hauled our designated starter log to a local sawmill. There are several of these small operations, haphazard outposts of industry tucked back in the woods here and there. Pungent mounds of sawdust, as high as houses, are their only advertisement, and business procedures are informal.

On a hot August afternoon I pulled into the mill yard with my one-log load and waited until the sawyer acknowledged my presence. I respectfully approached and told him I needed to have my log split exactly in half, lengthwise. He looked skeptical, but I knew he was used to oddball orders. With the help of two of his relatives who doubled as part-time employees, we hefted the log onto skids and rolled it to the saw carriage. The twenty-three-footer just barely fit into his shed. He dogged it securely and then eased the carriage up to the three-foot circular blade. "Like this?" he said, as he lined up the gleaming teeth. We eyeballed the log together, imagining the path of the blade and how the halves should fall apart. He tilted the log a fraction of an inch to the left. "Like this?" On custom jobs the final responsibility rests with the customer; and there are no refunds.

The log was fairly straight, but it tapered dramatically from butt to top, and it was not immediately obvious that a saw kerf begun at the middle of the big end would emerge near the middle of the small end. The result might be one half log (more or less) and one slab of wood suitable for kindling. There were no optics, lasers, or computers to guide us, so I just looked at it for a while.

Finally, I bravely said, "Looks good," and the saw started to scream. The carriage fed our log to the blade, and the shiny blur howled through it in a matter of seconds. At the end the log popped in two, and the pieces really were halves, or close enough to it. "Looks good," I said.

It was sweltering inside that shed, and the sawyer was dripping with sweat when I asked him what I owed for the cut. He stared at the half logs and scratched his head, figuring.

"How about an ice-cold six-pack?" he replied. I went off and found him one.

Looking two courses up from where the starter log now rests, I see the log that was notched by our friend from Chicago. He had ventured north for a visit just as the log work was getting underway, and I dragged him out to the homesite to lend a hand. I convinced him it was recreation.

He was working as a CPA and computer whiz for a major accounting firm and knew nothing of chain saws and wood chisels. His kind of chips were all micro. I assumed he would butcher a notch, but it would be a nice slice of experience for him and we had a few extra logs.

I set up a log for notching, helped him mark the cut with a scribe, administered a quick saw and chisel lesson, and turned him loose. All afternoon he labored over the log, repeatedly rolling it to and fro, checking and rechecking his progress. I could picture him huddled over his ledgers and terminals, fastidiously "chipping" away with the same concentrated intensity, the same passion for accuracy and completion. It was obvious this account was going to be in order; and he wasn't going to hack off any fingers either.

When the CPA finally rolled the log into place for the last time, it settled with the pleasant *thunk* that signifies a good fit. That city slicker's notch fit as fine as any in the structure. Even accountants can be trained to perform productive work.

Looking four courses up the wall from what I'll always know as the "CPA's entry," I see the distinctly curved and knotted log I was notching when I fell through the chimney hole.

Our masonry chimney would eventually rise out of the basement, through the house, and reach for the sky, but at that point there was only a foundation in the cellar and a 1½-by-2-foot opening in the subfloor. I had prudently covered the hole with a scrap of plywood to prevent an inadvertent display of slapstick, but the shades of Laurel and Hardy wouldn't rest. One day, for reasons now lost to me (and probably astray then, as well), the innocent hole was uncovered, transformed from a legitimate structural feature into a gaping mantrap.

I had just finished the notch and dropped the log into position. I backed away to inspect my work and stepped into the hole. As my left leg plunged straight down into nothingness, I mused upon the disadvantages of stupidity. Fortunately, the right leg did not follow. I was partially wedged into the hole for a moment, crying out in pain, embarrassment, and surprise. I had an ugly scrape on my thigh and a couple of severely pulled muscles. I struggled out of the opening and lay on the floor, writhing and grunting in pain.

The dog usually slept in a sunny corner while I worked, and he was aroused by the commotion. He padded over, gave me a perfunctory sniff, and ambled off. Apparently he was satisfied I would live; no Rin Tin Tin that one. It was nice I hadn't broken a leg—I just couldn't picture him tearing off down the road in a frantic, frothing search for the nearest paramedic.

No, his niche is there by the wood stove, especially when the snow starts to pile up. But I don't think he slumbers quite as blissfully as he used to—Bloody Alice has seen to that. When she's curled up in your lap, sleeping the sleep of the arrogant, the cat seems harmless enough, almost benign. But it's only a ploy, another diversion designed to set up the dog for further humiliation.

We became aware of this a couple of winters ago when we were all gathered around the stove on a cold February night. The dog was spread out in his customary spot, all four legs languidly extended, his snout buried in the rug. He hadn't stirred for a long time.

Alice rose from my lap, quietly dropped to the floor, and gracefully stretched. She sat for a moment, licking her paws and washing her face. Then she walked nonchalantly past the dog and stopped behind him, just a few inches from his rump. She stared at him for a moment and then flopped over on her side, precisely mimicking his position. The dog still slept. Alice reached out with her front legs, talons bared, and dug into the dog's fur. His eyes snapped open. I thought he would jump up, but I saw his legs stiffen where they lay. The hundred-pound dog was paralyzed by the three-pound cat.

Slowly Alice began to work her way up the dog's back, pulling herself along with her claws. The dog whimpered, and his eyes rolled back, trying to catch sight of this demon. His paws twitched nervously, but he made no effort to rise and flee.

Finally Alice arrived at the back of the dog's head, and with a deft flick of her right paw, she flopped the retriever's ear over to one side. His whimper turned into a whine and he stared at me, pleading for help. But I was enthralled by the cat's audacity and the dog's obvious fear; I was anxious to see what the devious feline had in mind.

In a moment she began to gently lick the sensitive inside of the dog's ear. It was tender and affectionate attention, and it must have felt good, because the dog instantly relaxed, closed his eyes, and started softly grunting with pleasure. Alice caressed the pink tissues with her tongue for a full minute, lulling the dog into a calm and happy state. Then, with a swift thrust of her head, she viciously sank her fangs into the delicate skin. The dog leaped up and howled, his tail between his legs. I sprang up to grab him before he bashed his panic-stricken weight into the furniture, and he cowered in fear of me, knowing he wasn't supposed to raise hell in the house. Everybody had it in for him.

As I calmed the dog, Bloody Alice sat in the kitchen, placidly licking her paws and ignoring us both. It had been the perfect sting. From then on the dog always watched her closely, especially if she tried to move behind him. He would get up and guard himself until she was out of his sight and then ease back into fitful sleep with the greatest of caution. He was old, but he'd learned a new trick.

And he wasn't the only one. I doubt I'll ever allow the cat to nuzzle my ear. We've learned a lot from animals over the years. I recall the autumn afternoon I drove up to the house and caught sight of Pam standing on the back porch, clutching the .410 shotgun and trembling with rage. Scattered about the yard in broken, feathery heaps were the carcasses of thirty chickens. Our eight-month-old husky crouched sheepishly by the porch, feathers pasted on his lips.

Pam, a caring and sensitive lover of animals whom I once saw weep at the death of a sparrow, had bloody slaughter in her eyes. The only reason the dog still lived was that she couldn't find any ammunition. It's shocking how chickens can transform your personality.

When you live in the woods you quickly realize that your life is inextricably intertwined with the lives and deaths of many animals, domestic and wild. It's easy to find yourself in complex symbiotic relationships. We provide food, water, shelter, medication, leftovers, and love to the dog, and in turn he intercepts wood ticks, porcupine quills, and skunk scent that might otherwise have afflicted us. He also relieves us of the burden of butchering chickens. Admittedly, our benefits from this symbiosis are subtle, but we had once entertained higher hopes. We had hoped that the dog would intercept bears.

One night when I was away and the dog was automatically on duty, Pam was awakened by the sound of one of the beehives being unceremoniously splintered. A large black bear had dropped by for a snack. The bees, somewhat irritated, raised a frightful buzz, but there was no sound of heroic barking. With two hives in ruins, the bear knocked over the garbage can, broke down a fruit tree, dug a pit in the garden (for some buried fish heads we'd interred for fertilizer), and as a final insult finished off the Purina in the dog's dish. Finally, Pam, that caring and sensitive lover of all animals, scared the bear off with a blast from the .410.

The next morning I found the dog ambling down the road a couple of miles from the house. I gave him a lift home. As soon as we wheeled into the yard he caught a whiff of the bear. Leaping from the truck, hackles high, he sprinted to the garbage can to see what the bear had overlooked. Finished there, he bravely pranced around the fragments of the beehives and confidently barked three times. He then strode to his dish, and finding it empty, favored me with an accusing glance. How's a dog supposed to intercept bears on an empty stomach?

We soon discovered that raccoons were his forte, for one night he treed one in a birch just outside our extra bedroom, barking and yelping, barking and yelping. We were hosting some extremely tired guests who had driven fifteen hundred miles and badly needed rest, so I went outside and dragged the dog into the house. I figured the raccoon would leave during the night. By morning the coon had indeed departed, but the dog refused to be fooled. He immediately returned to the base of the tree and resumed barking. I tried to reason with him. I grabbed his head, pointed it toward the top of the tree, and whispered threatening obscenities in his ear. I tried to distract him with treats and toys. Nothing worked; he had raccoon fever. Even his usual nemesis, a whack with a rolled-up newspaper, was only temporarily effective. He barked, off and on, all day.

As darkness approached with the promise of another long, loud night I finally gave in to passion. I grabbed the chain saw, and while the dog watched expectantly, his ears perked, I cut down the tree.

"See?" I yelled. "The coon is gone, you SOB."

The dog jumped into the fallen branches, briefly sniffed around, then briefly lifted his leg. Satisfied, he walked over to his bed and curled up to sleep—his work was finished at last. For a menacing moment my finger tightened on the chain saw's trigger.

We had better luck with Alice. She was the runt of her litter, and we drafted her for that very reason. We wanted an aggressive cat, an enthusiastic mouser, and we figured that since Alice was so small she'd go through her nine lives with a chip on her haunch, always trying to make up for her size. I'd had a short boyhood pal who grew up with a tall sister, and he'd spent the bulk of his adolescence beating up other kids. I wasn't sure whether that kind of motivation applied to cats, but it was worth a try.

The first autumn after the cat took over the house, several dozen field mice decided to spend the winter indoors. Our kitchen cabinets apparently served as a rodent's equivalent of a condo in Miami. Bloody Alice quickly became the equivalent of a tidal wave. Within several weeks we were able to credit her with twenty-three kills. And she made certain she got credit. She'd stage a show every time she caught a mouse, dribbling and batting the noxious little fur balls around the kitchen floor before dispatching them. Then, after a decent interval, she would ceremoniously drop the half-eaten mice at our feet. It was nice, at first, to see the vermin being terminated, but the entertainment value declined rapidly.

By spring the vacationing mice were wiped out, and we were ready for Alice to move outdoors for the summer. She happily obliged, casting her murderous eyes upon the dangerous chickadees and wood warblers who frequent our yard. But their gift of flight stymied Bloody Alice, and soon she turned her attention to other game.

One morning in late May, as Pam and I worked at planting our garden, the cat came out to see what she could flush from the tall grass at the edge of the yard. She slunk along the ground a few feet in front of us, then suddenly dropped into a crouch, her eyes aglow with blood lust, her body tensed for the fatal spring. She was focused on something behind us. We turned to follow her gaze and there, only twenty feet away, were two white-tailed deer, about two hundred pounds apiece.

Pam, our caring and sensitive lover of all animals, said, "Go for it, Alice! There's room in the freezer." But the deer bounded off, and Alice, catching us staring at her, lazily licked a paw and assumed the feline air of eternal boredom.

We encouraged Alice to loiter around the garden and prey upon the mice that liked to nibble on our beets. I also hoped her formidable presence would deter the blue jays who loved to pluck our tender young corn shoots from the ground and devour what remained of the germinated seed. But the corn was too delicious for the jays to stay away, and Alice, not sharing our love of fresh sweet corn, seemed to lack motivation for the job. She'd lost interest in birds with their cowardly wings.

As row after row of our precious corn disappeared and the time for replanting slipped quickly away, I desperately searched the gardening literature for an alternative solution. The books agreed that one of the best ways to fight animals is with other animals (that's why you need at least two political parties), or at least with the appearance of other animals. To me, the most promising suggestion of the lot was to construct a giant spider web. Birds are supposed to avoid webs. So I got a roll of twine and some stakes, and with the aid of my friend Sooch (scuttling back and forth like an arachnid) wove a four-hundred-square-foot "web" about one foot above the corn patch. We laughed and shook our heads when we finished, but the damn thing actually worked—for about five days. The jays weren't that stupid.

Sooch then suggested his sweet old grandmother's remedy for thieving birds: shoot a couple of the offenders and hang their bodies in the garden for all to see. He claimed that this avian terrorism never failed, but I lacked the stomach for jackboot gardening.

I decided to cut the jays in on a piece of the action that year, but over the winter an item in a seed catalog caught my eye. The following spring I unveiled my secret weapon: an inflatable plastic owl. Kinky, but effective. I tied "Hooty" to a tall stake, and every morning and evening I moved him (or her, it's hard to tell) to a different spot in the garden to give the illusion of life. The jays have taken their piracy elsewhere.

Still, such successes in the zoological sphere seem to be rare. After Pam failed to shoot our fowl-hungry husky, I tried a traditional remedy. I hooked the dog on a short leash, tied one of the chicken carcasses around his neck, and left him there to contemplate the rotting corpse for two days, without food. This unkind gesture was supposed to instill a pathological aversion to chicken meat. The dog whined and cried for a time, and then slept. And then, after the two days, when the chicken was good and ripe, the dog ate it—with relish, it seemed to me.

So before we procured more chickens we gave the husky away, writing him off as worthless. But to be fair, he had intercepted a lot of ticks.

Chickens, of course, are an embarrassment. We nurtured a small flock for three years and found they are incompatible with genteel backwoods living. Anyone who respects intelligence would rather feed the squirrels and skunks.

Chickens are as bright and quick as axe handles, and I know only one person who was ever seriously entertained by their behavior. He was a city boy and our flock ambushed him one evening.

Pam had just landed a job at a newspaper in town, and after a suitable probation period she invited her editor and his wife out for dinner. We had planned a barbeque and it rained, so I dragged the grill into the garage and the editor and I got acquainted out there, sipping beer and guarding the steaks.

The beer did its purgative work, and I told the editor he could just step behind the garage to relieve himself—no sense in walking all the way into the house just to use the bathroom. One of the great conveniences of rural life is that you are free to urinate in the yard if you want to. ("Yard" is a euphemism. A "yard" is a cleared space for a septic tank drainfield, and a grazing area for deer and rabbits. Do not picture a manicured lawn. To say something is "out in the yard" does not necessarily pinpoint its location. "Yards" tend to bleed off into the woods for indeterminate distances. If I say I spotted a moose "in our backyard," it may have been on the neighboring forty.)

Anyway, the editor slipped out in back of the garage, and in a little while I heard loud laughter, cackling peels of unrestrained mirth. Hm, I thought, this dude really knows how to entertain himself; and when he returned to grillside I favored him with a skeptical look. He was still chuckling as he reported his adventure.

He had gone behind the garage and unzipped his fly right in front of our fenced-in chicken yard. Our thirty Rhode Island Reds, who had just enough savvy to get in out of the rain (sometimes) were holed up in their coop.

But as the editor added his small stream to the soft din of the splattering rain, one of the hens poked her head around the corner of the coop doorway and stared at him. A second head shot out from the other side, then a third from the first side, then a fourth—all staring at him. He giggled, self-conscious about being self-conscious while exposed before hens. But after all, they were females. He giggled again.

That was enough for the chickens. This was obviously a human, and perhaps he had chicken feed. In a squawking flurry, the whole herd of thirty Reds burst out of the coop and charged up to the fence. They crowded in front of the editor, cocking their heads to and fro, jiggling their crops as they clucked and stared. This is when he laughed, trying to keep the stream off his shoes. Never had he enjoyed such a captivated, appreciative audience. There was an immediacy that is lacking on the op-ed page.

I was glad the chickens had helped to entertain our guest, but it didn't erase the bitter memory of what they'd done to our canoe.

It was in the autumn, time to butcher the Reds and establish them in the freezer where they belonged. I eased into the chicken yard, distracting my future fryers with a deceptive shower of feed. It was relatively simple to grab the first victim and spirit her off to the block, and I must admit I felt zero remorse as I swung the hatchet.

But the rest of the Reds grew a tad suspicious, and my second foray into the yard was an embarrassing fiasco. Though not brilliant, chickens are fleet of foot, nimble of feather, and hold strong opinions about decapitation. They were soon running around like chickens with their heads still on, and I was lurching after them, clutching at air and cursing.

There had to be a better way, and I concluded that it resided in the clip of my .22 rifle. Besides, it was more humane and in closer accord with the methods of the twentieth century. I stood silently outside the fence, where the chickens assumed I was harmless, and I had all the time I needed to draw a careful bead on the head of a hen. I squeezed off a round and she expired instantly—no muss, no fuss. Well, maybe a little muss.

The other Reds were unflustered, not able to grasp the modern concept of long-range doom. One by one I picked off the whole flock, and it was much less traumatic for all concerned than if I'd flailed away with a bloody, feather-plastered axe.

The only problem (besides the subsequent horror of plucking) was that one of the .22 rounds had passed through a chicken, through the coop, and through the hull of our canoe, which I had forgotten was parked behind the coop in the field of fire. I had won the battle but lost the war. Oh, nefarious chickens!

It was nice to be supplied with large homemade eggs (double-yolked as often as not), but the novelty of poultry husbandry wore off quickly, especially when we once tried to keep a flock through the winter. We filled the coop with hay and installed an infrared lamp (which cost us more to run than we got for the eggs), but still their water would freeze solid on a regular basis. Twice a day in January I'd take the car tire half that served as their trough and slam it on the ground until the chunks of water fell out. I'd then refill it and hope the Reds got enough to drink before it recrystallized.

One particularly frigid morning I entered the coop and found that one of the hens had apparently crystallized as well. She was lying on her back with her legs sticking straight up. They were swollen to twice their diameter and had turned from pale yellow to a shocking green. I figured she was dead, but then she opened an eye and uttered a speculative, slightly pathetic cluck.

Being opposed to subzero weather, Pam was immediately empathetic and suggested we bring the hen into our kitchen to see if we could thaw her out. I assumed it was a heroic, futile effort, but I was wrong.

We placed the chicken in a towel-lined cardboard box next to the warm stove, and in an hour she was back to normal, hopping around the room on two good yellow legs. I was amazed by her toughness and resilience, and as a reward I reintroduced her to the coop. She was just growing accustomed to the kitchen, and if a Rhode Island Red can look disappointed, this one did. Now that she'd seen how the masters lived, I hoped she wouldn't become a rabble-rousing subversive, convincing the layers to strike and inciting the rooster to peck at my ankles.

But fortunately, I've never seen an axe handle revolt either, and the coop remained peaceful, locked up in a smelly universe of soiled hay and ignorant complacency. There's a lesson in that for all of us. As E. B. White once wrote: "I don't know what's more discouraging, literature or chickens."

Well, I vote for chickens—better read than Reds.

While it's easy to be rid of chickens, I learned that a bear, especially if it happens to be dead, is not so easily managed. My friend Mike inadvertently exposed me to this truth.

He didn't want to kill that bear, but what could he do? He wasn't too keen on the idea of losing all his beehives either. The black bear, a three-hundred-pound male, had his head fully crammed into Mike's second hive. The first hive lay in a shambles, a scattered ruin of cracked boxes and shattered frames. Tens of thousands of enraged bees were swarming around the bear, frightening and impressive to us but of little account to the bear. He had honey on his mind (and on his nose, paws, ears, and tongue) and could not be distracted. It seemed that observing wildlife at close range was going to be one of the perks associated with raising bees in the backwoods.

Mike, a retired mine foreman, was used to dealing with personnel problems. He first tried the old trick of banging pots together, but seriously, folks, has anyone ever actually seen this work? It was a mere formality. He didn't really expect a creature which could blithely ignore legions of grief-stricken bees to pay any mind to a couple of tinny kitchen utensils. It probably wouldn't have worked with miners either.

Mike then shouted at the bear: loud and impolite words which would have provoked or dismayed most other creatures. A miner, for example, might have responded with violence, or at least a few rude gestures. But Yogi was unmoved. He was up to his small, twitching ears in dessert. It was late spring, and after a winter in the sack he was *hungry,* ravenous in a way we can only imagine. Maybe it's an aching desire akin to the pangs of the camper who's been in the bush gobbling dehydrated food for a week, and who, when he finally hits the streets again, does grateful obeisance at the foot of the golden arches. Who knows?

There was still a third hive intact, and Mike felt he had only one alternative. He phoned the local game warden, hastily explained the situation, and obtained permission to shoot the bear. It was distasteful, but he had too much time and money invested in those bees. He loaded his 12-gauge shotgun with a slug and crept up behind the feasting bear. With the muzzle almost touching fur, he fired one shot and the bear died instantly. Mike heaved a sigh of relief. The last thing he needed was a *wounded* hungry bear. The matter of the hives could well have become academic.

So, there was a large dead bear lying in the grass. Presently the bees would calm and console themselves, and then what? Mike asked me if I wanted the bear; he wasn't going to do anything with it. Well, I hated to see it go to waste, so I said, sure, I'd take it. I'd never dressed out a bear before, but I didn't imagine it could be too difficult. Silly boy.

I called my friend Dick, whose chief qualifications for the task were that he was nearby and available. He did, however, have a certain empathy for the bear. He'd once been the starting goalie for the Notre Dame hockey team, and he knows what it feels like to be shot at and hit. When it came to skinning, he was also inexperienced, but we got some knives and went at it with the gusto engendered by ignorance.

There were no trees or poles nearby which we might have employed to hang the carcass conveniently and thus make the job easier, and it didn't seem practical to drag the ponderous thing for some distance to the woods. So we decided to butcher it right there on the lawn, and quickly discovered it was going to be much more difficult than we'd expected.

We had visions of a bearskin rug lying before a fireplace, and so we were determined to be fastidious with the hide. Since neither one of us is very good at structural visualization, we had to be constantly rolling the carcass over to ensure that our cuts were going to result in a hide which resembled a bear and not a hairy black blanket with ears. The bear was surprisingly heavy and awkward, and shoving it around became a sweaty chore. Then, with my first few inept slices, I stupidly cut the skin all the way around one of the paws, thereby separating it and its claws from the rest of the hide. Well, we figured, that could be sewn back on later.

But it was only the beginning of sorrows. With a slip of the knife Dick did the same thing to another paw. So we decided, for the sake of symmetry, to just hack them all off and worry about it later. This unfortunate decision led to other sloppiness, and soon we were bloody and gory up to our armpits, and growing more frustrated by the minute. It was approaching dusk and we weren't even half done.

It was then that a doctor showed up. An acquaintance of Dick's, he was a surgeon at the hospital in town. He'd dropped by to visit and was informed that Dick was at the neighbor's, skinning a bear. He surveyed our handiwork with some amusement and offered to lend a hand, though he said he'd never dressed out a bear either. I was skeptical, not least for the fact that he was attired in fine clothes: expensive white slacks and spotless white shirt and shoes. Our clothes by this time were a bloody mess. Someone giving the scene a cursory glance might have concluded that we were the ones being dressed out.

I mentioned this, but the good doctor shrugged it off. It soon became apparent that there was no need for concern. He took my semi-sharp knife, and in his surgeon's hands it was transformed into a sure and effective scalpel. Dick and I watched in admiring amazement as he began to execute deft and speedy cuts with, yes, surgical precision. He took that bear apart. In a jiffy the rest of the hide was off. That done, it seemed only a matter of moments before the abdominal cavity was exposed and the doctor was delivering a running commentary, an anatomy lecture, as he happily sliced away. I felt like a witness at an autopsy.

Under his direction we helped him here and there, getting the flavor of a surgical nurse's job. In about twenty minutes the job was done, and the doctor stepped back to admire his work. His white duds were still impeccable. Only the tips of his fingers were bloodied.

"I could have done better with a sharp knife," he said, and went into the house to wash up.

We ended up with a lot of bear meat, and the reviews were mixed. I liked it, though I must admit it possesses a strong odor and a very wild taste. The key is to disguise it in some way. Mary corned a batch of it, using a recipe for corned beef, and it was delightful. Smothering it with barbeque sauce also did the trick. I found that many Indian tribes had taboos against eating bear. I presume this arose because, like its relative the hog, the bear is subject to trichinosis, which can be passed on to humans with fatal results. You must make certain the meat is well cooked. I noticed that our dog, usually a voracious and omnivorous chowhound, would not touch bear meat, cooked or raw. I don't intend to touch raw bear again either, unless of course there's a competent surgeon handy.

As I said, Mike didn't want to kill that bear, and most people I know would rather see wild animals alive than dead. Many humans will try to aid an animal in distress, even if it means inconvenience, and sometimes danger, to themselves. For example, the predicament of a trio of baby birds recently impelled me to make an extreme effort that in turn was impelled by a debt to a fellow human being. The story goes back to 1962.

I remember the pattern of the clouds. It was the last thing I saw before sinking beneath the waves and losing consciousness. The lifeguard plucked me off the bottom of the lake, and when I came to, I felt the vivifying sensation of being pushed rapidly toward shore by large, strong hands. Above, the summer clouds were still floating, puffy white cumulus in a sunny blue sky. I was eleven years old and I'd never seen anything so beautiful.

But I also remember the terrible liquid in my lungs, the sickening panic as the water first strangled me and then slowly gave way beneath my thrashing legs and buried me alive. I attained a crisp, nightmarish understanding of the term "watery grave." It was this understanding that forced me, twenty-three years later, to plunge from the safe and comfortable deck of a pontoon boat into cold, deep, weed-choked water. It was an unplanned swim.

Pam and our friend Nancy had commandeered her father's pontoon. It was the July Fourth weekend and beautiful weather. Making the most of this unusual circumstance, we filled a cooler with pop and beer, grabbed two fishing rods and one novel, and set out for a cruise on Big Sturgeon Lake.

Nancy's father had rushed the boat into the water in early May, the first one on the lake after the ice went out, and then, as usual, it had remained idle at the dock for seven weeks. Naturally enough, the Johnson outboard motor had grown resentful and refused to start. Repeated flicks of the ignition switch produced only a series of anemic coughs. But sunshine and sparkling water beckoned, and we would not be easily deterred from our patriotic quest of an enjoyable Fourth. We popped the cover on the motor and dug out a starter rope. The manufacturers of outboards understand the fickleness of batteries and charging systems, and so I confidently wrapped the rope around the flywheel supplied for that purpose. On the count of three, I yanked the rope and Nancy hit the ignition. We were rewarded by a brief growl of encouragement from the Johnson. It obviously appreciated this special attention after a half season of neglect. With less than a dozen pulls the motor roared into action.

I took the helm while Pam and Nancy readied their fishing tackle and directed me to one of their "hot spots." The water was choppy and some dark thunderheads were building slowly and magnificently off to the east, but the breeze was warm and the lake seemed friendly and benign. When we reached the appointed weed bed, about a hundred yards off a wooded peninsula, I cut back the engine to a nice trolling crawl and attempted to follow the course outlined by the women. However, those two are fanatical anglers, scornful of flippant, trifling fishermen such as myself, and the navigation was not up to their standards of precision. (It was as good an excuse as any for the lack of bites.)

Pam took over the wheel and I gladly settled into a chair, put my feet up, and burrowed into the novel. It was *The Haj* by Leon Uris, and soon I was snaking through the sunbaked caves at Qumran, hiding from the Bedouin and meditating upon the suras of the Koran. I was far away from Big Sturgeon Lake and unprepared for the trauma to come. Meanwhile, Pam and Nancy decided to find a "hole" and drop anchor. When the appropriate spot had been pinpointed, Nancy leaned over the bow to free the anchor rope and tie it to the anchor. It was secured to a pulley under the lip of the deck, and as she pulled it free she let out a stricken, mournful wail. "Oh no!"

I was instantly transported from the deserts of the Middle East.

"What's the matter?" Pam cried.

Nancy pointed to the water, close to tears. "I dumped some baby birds into the lake!"

And there they were, three tiny swallows, fluffy and feathery, beating their fragile wings against the cold water. Their nest had been constructed on top of the pulley, completely under the boat deck and out of sight. When Nancy jerked the rope, the mud and straw nest had been ripped apart and the terrified birds tumbled into the lake. We all lunged for the rail and stretched out to grab the hapless nestlings, but they were just out of reach, peeping frantically and desperately flapping to stay afloat. I held on to Pam as she leaned out past the point of balance in a valiant effort, but to no avail. In seconds we drifted several feet away. Pam uttered a pitiful "Ooooh," like someone keening at a wake. "We've got to get them!" she cried.

The motor wouldn't start. Nancy, ever the dedicated angler and trying to put the best face on things, mentioned weakly that the young birds would make a tasty meal for some growing northern pike. True, the tender young lives would not be totally wasted, but before they entered the food chain they would probably drown. And they were not passing softly into death. Their peeps and squeaks, usually the sweet music of early summer mornings, sounded now like shrieks of horror as they called in vain for mama.

"We've got to get them!" Pam cried again. I grabbed an oar and tried to reach one with that, but couldn't come close. I realized then that I couldn't bear to see anything drown. Even two decades later the memory of my own panic was much too vivid. I peeled off shirt, shoes, and glasses and clambered over the rail and onto a pontoon. I crouched there a moment, establishing a firm footing on the slippery aluminum, and then flopped into the water.

By now the closest swallow was about twenty feet away, and I breaststroked through the chop, head up, so I wouldn't lose sight of it. Slimy weeds clutched at my wrists and ankles. As I closed in I extended my arm, cupped my hand, and lifted the bird clear of the water as gently as I could. The puny talons instantly tried to grip my flesh and hang on. Then, with the bird raised over my head and stroking with the other arm, I kicked madly for the boat. The wind was blowing it farther away, and Pam and Nancy, each with an oar, fought hard to keep it as near as possible.

I handed the first survivor to Pam, who immediately wrapped it in her blouse. I hoisted myself partway onto a pontoon to get a bearing on the next bird. Without my glasses it was just a fuzzy speck on the crest of a wave. Nancy pointed, and I shoved off, hoping the birds could stay buoyant for a few minutes longer. I was surprised they hadn't already gone under. I scooped up the second survivor in the same manner as the first, and had to swim a good distance for the third, but we rescued them all.

We got the motor started, and as we raced back to shore, Pam cuddled the shivering little bodies, trying to give them warmth. We moored the boat in the exact spot it had been in since May, hoping the parents would resume their duties. Nancy knew of an abandoned nest near her father's outhouse, and she brought it down to the lake. I couldn't place the new nest in the same location as the original because that one had been stuck to a vertical aluminum surface bit by bit with the swallows' own adhesive. So instead I laid it on top of the port pontoon, just a couple of feet away and still sheltered by the deck. We used duct tape, one of the few truly indispensable components of modern civilization, to attach the nest to the pontoon. It looked ridiculous, but it was secure.

Then I eased the babies, one by one, into their new home. The hardest part was convincing them to release their frightened grip on Pam's blouse. They'd apparently grown leery of change. We left the area for about an hour, and then Nancy cautiously returned to see how things were going. She saw two adult swallows perched on the pontoon and fussing over the nest. Our heroic efforts had not been in vain, though the parents, no doubt, were now somewhat cynical about boats.

I don't know what the memory of birds is like, if they can recall the pattern of the clouds. But I do remember, and I was pleased to at least partially return the favor of a lifeguard from long ago. In saving me, he can be gratified to know that he also saved three swallows.

But just because you don't often kill animals doesn't mean you don't often hunt. I remember the day there was a deer in our garden. We saw it from the living room window. She'd already eaten the two remaining cabbages; the rest of the crops had long since been harvested. The sleek young doe was now picking at clumps of grass, their blades white with hard November frost.

We'd been off traveling for two weeks, and the deer had apparently grown accustomed to the quiet emptiness of the yard. The din of human activity had faded back into the comforting ambience of the forest. Of course the succulent cabbages had probably also helped to overcome her native shyness.

We had a few frames of color film left in the camera, so I screwed on a telephoto lens and crept out the back door. The doe couldn't see the porch steps from the garden, but the ears of deer are like supersensitive sonar, alert to every nuance of vibration. I slithered down the stairs as softly as I could, but the second step creaked under my weight—sharp, high-pitched, and loud. Or so it seemed. Surely the doe would bolt. But when I reached the corner of the house and took a peek, she was still there feeding, about fifty feet away. It was windy, so there was a lot of background noise—rustling and shaking in the trees—and that probably saved me.

Braced against the logs, I eased the Pentax up to my face, set the zoom lens at 135 mm, and focused on her right eye. I could only count on one shot—the sound of the shutter might scare her off. I sucked in a breath, let half of it out, and had my finger on the release when she took a step forward to reach some fresh grass. Rats! Her head and neck were now obscured by a small balsam tree which grew in the yard between us. Still peering through the lens, I watched her tail jiggle, and debated. If I tried to sneak out into the yard and get a better angle, the doe would certainly see me and blast off before I could shoot. I could take the shot I now had—admittedly not the best—but it would show a deer in our garden and would look nice on the screen. The odds were, however, that it would be the only picture I got.

I decided that a deer in the viewfinder was worth two in the imagination, so I gently squeezed the shutter release. *Click! Clack!* Or so it sounded to me. Her head shot up. The balsam concealed all but her ears, and they twitched, seeking out the echoes and frequencies of danger. I froze, the camera still pressed to my face, and in a moment she resumed grazing. So I was lucky. I had one shot "in the can" and could now afford to gamble. If I took it slow and kept the balsam between us, I might have a chance of creeping into a better position. I recalled the animal-observing advice given me by a friend: Don't act like a carnivore. He once encountered a deer nearly face to face in the woods, and he stayed within a few feet of it for several minutes by pretending to be a fellow herbivore. The deer was pulling leaves off the surrounding brush, so my friend did the same, ripping them off the branches with his teeth and chewing them for a while. The deer would eat, and then he would "eat," and at times they'd eat together. The whitetail was satisfied with this. If this strange bipedal leaf-eater was not exactly a friend, neither was he an obvious foe. But I didn't think that strategy would work here. I was carrying a "weapon"—a shiny, alien artifact made out of glass and metal, something that "shoots." Herbivores don't carry cameras.

I edged away from the corner of the cabin and lined up with the tree. It was roughly halfway to the garden, and I thought if I could reach it undetected, I might poke the lens through the upper boughs and obtain an excellent shot.

The ground was littered with dry, brown autumn leaves, as

crisp as potato chips. The sound of a shutter might confuse the doe, but she definitely knew the sound of a crushed leaf, and stepping on one of those would end the game instantly. I started to do a slow and complicated waltz across the lawn, gingerly placing my boots alongside, between, and around the brittle leaves. I paused after each short step, the Pentax at chest level, my eyes divided between the doe and the ground. She continued to pull at the grass. Fortunately I was downwind, or my scent would no doubt have betrayed me.

I was two yards away from the balsam when I blew it. I stepped on a leaf and it crunched like an eggshell. The rustle of the wind in the woods was no help this time. The doe's head shot up again and her whole body tensed for a spring. She stared directly at the balsam, trying to make out the threat. I stared back at her through the branches, motionless and holding my breath. We were less than twenty feet apart, peering at each other through the needles, but she was unsure. For several seconds it was a standoff. I dared not blink, much less raise the camera to my eye. The doe was like a raw nerve—the slightest stimulus would cause an explosion. She knew there was something behind the tree, but I was camouflaged by the foliage. We stared.

I didn't realize it, but Pam had followed behind me, stalking us both. She stepped on a leaf. The doe kicked straight up, her hindquarters high, and then vaulted fifteen feet across the garden in a graceful arc, a yard off the ground. Her front hooves hit the grass and she seemed to bounce off her back legs, bounding into the brush, chest-high, between two aspens. Her white flag of a tail flashed and she was gone. It happened in three seconds, and I didn't get a shot.

That is, not with the camera. But I can still see the doe in mid-flight, stretching out for the safety of the forest. Her coat is thick and glossy, briefly catching the flat rays of the late autumn sun. Her head is high, nose pointed at the horizon in a royal angle of mastery. She doesn't need antlers to demonstrate her magnificence. The tall white tail is straight up, like a counterweight to the elegant, muscular neck, while her legs are comfortably bent, braced and cocked for the next sinewy burst of power. Her hard black hooves are nimble and light. Wings would be redundant, a color slide unfit.

SEVEN
The Quest and the Kill

There is a time for rifles. Though I've never met a deer I wanted to kill, I couldn't pass up the novelty (in this day and age) of a canoe-wilderness moose hunt. It seemed like something a person who lives in a log cabin should do, at least once.

I can picture the ornate calligraphy on the parchment for The Exalted Northwoods Rites of Initiation into the Amateur Order of Frontier People. It reads:

1. *Construct cabin* (native trees).
2. *Muse in front of wood stove* (Lincolnesque thoughts).
3. *Hunt moose* (surviving to muse further).
4. *Eat moose* (food for thought).
5. *Return to city* (enlightened).

Wreathed with antlers and suitable for framing, the document could go for $18.95 during the summer tourist infestation.

The moose hunt cost us a bit more than that.

Many a dubious enterprise has been justified on the grounds that it will provide "something to tell your grandchildren"—the assumption being that you'll live that long. If you aim to collect a lot of stories for your grandchildren, you'd be well advised to write them down, just in case. Still, we must have adventure, and it's never killed anyone who survived it. At least half the fun comes from the tales told, of course, and so it is with the Delta Lake Moose Hunt. A true story. I have witnesses.

Getting the chance to hunt moose in Minnesota is something of an adventure in itself. First of all, you have to be lucky. Permits are distributed by lottery every other year. A hunting party of four pays $140 for the privilege of taking one moose, and your chances of paying for that privilege are about one in twenty. Mike, Gerry, Mick, and I were among the twelve hundred parties whose hopes were vindicated one year.

Mike, a farm boy turned engineer, brimming with practical ideas, hunting experience, and the engineer's can-do arrogance, was our more or less acknowledged leader. Gerry was our concession to a generation that, let's face it, has seen its better days. He's in his fifties, but fit, and a seasoned deer hunter. Gutting big game in the bush is a routine operation for Gerry— strictly outpatient work. Having entered every lottery since it began in 1971, he was thrilled with his belated good fortune in 1983. Twelve years is a long time to dream about anything, even moose.

Mick and I came up smelling like roses in our first lottery, much to the disgust of some passionate hunter friends of ours who had been disappointed for years and detected a different odor. Though we are avid backwoods types, Mick and I could only be described as greenhorns when it came to big-game hunting. When we heard a permit was ours, Mick bought a used rifle and I borrowed one. Tacky, very tacky.

All moose hunters, regardless of experience, must attend an orientation session. Mick and I took one in Ely, about an hour's drive north of Side Lake. The armed game wardens' presentation was part pep rally, part inquisition. They wished us luck in the hunt, but we were given to understand that the DNR (Department of Natural Resources) always gets its man. The warnings against misdeeds were so pointed, the tales of arrests so harrowing, that I wondered if maybe I had gotten the wrong impression about moose hunting being fun. I mean, maybe these dudes could call in an air strike or something. Having an acquired distaste for remedial measures, I resolved to toe the line. At the end of the long briefing, I expected someone to call out "Synchronize watches!" When no one did, we meekly filed out of the hall into a cold, pounding October rain.

Mike and Gerry were already encamped in the BWCA—the Boundary Waters Canoe Area wilderness—a million-acre non-motorized preserve along the Minnesota-Ontario border. They'd been properly oriented the day before. Mick and I were going in at 3:30 P.M., a scant three hours before sunset. Camp was four portages into the wilderness, but we figured we could make it before dark. We might have, too.

There we were, at the landing on Lake One. The canoe was in the water; our gear was ready to be stowed. I reached into the back of the truck for the paddles. When Mick saw me slumped over the side of the truck, moaning, he became alarmed.

"What's the matter with you?"

I told him, in language inappropriate for grandchildren.

Mick swore with real gusto. We threw the gear back into the truck and went careening up the road four or five miles to a resort on Snowbank Lake. There, for $4 apiece, we became the humble owners of two ragged, weather-beaten paddles. Nevertheless we blessed our good fortune. That outfitter could have charged us $20 apiece, and we would have paid, and he probably knew it. On the other hand, he must also have noticed that we were desperate and armed to the teeth. With such observations is prudence (and good business) nurtured.

With the chilling rain still falling, we pushed off into Lake One, bursting with an excited, childlike anticipation of the hunt. We were eager to pit ourselves against the rigors of the late-autumn wilderness, and our first challenge was upon us immediately. We didn't have a map for the first section of Lake One.

Navigating in the BWCA is generally a tricky business. Doing it without a map greatly simplifies matters. For the mapless, navigational decisions are reduced to an uncomplicated binary code, a fifty-fifty proposition. You go one way, or you go the other. At the Lake One landing, we found ourselves in a narrow channel. It appeared obvious we should go right, and we did, and we were wrong.

Our first portage was a dead giveaway: it was suspiciously pristine and underused. But we humped over it anyway and plopped the canoe into a natural labyrinth called, as a map would have told us, Confusion Lake. No doubt some early French adventurer had lost his soul in that life-size jigsaw puzzle of points and islands. We, however, were fired with the zeal of our mission—a mission that was fast becoming survival as our fears grew as dark as the ever-darkening overcast sky. We managed to bump our way across Confusion Lake and find the portage out. We were encouraged to find no skeletal remains lying about.

We paddled to the western end of Lake One and onto our map. We saw that we wouldn't have had to portage at all if we'd hung a left at the landing, and our confidence about reaching the campsite was waning. As we hit the portage out of One, the sun, mocking our pitiful human ambitions, shone briefly through the clouds, then promptly dropped below the wet horizon. So much for the great life-giver.

Just around a point off the portage into Lake Two, we came upon an enormous cow moose and two calves wading nonchalantly in the shallows not twenty yards from us. A good omen. The size of the cow was positively spine-tingling. Alas, the season didn't open until the next morning, and having acquired the fear of God, and His agents, the DNR, we didn't even dare look at our rifles. For their part, the moose were tremendously unimpressed with us. Judging by their lazy indifference, we must have occupied a status somewhere between that of mosquitoes and rabbit droppings.

We pressed on across Lake Two at a frantic clip. If we could find the next portage before dark (notice how adroitly we'd lowered our expectations), maybe we could still link up with Mike and Gerry. The darkness was coming faster. We located the general area where the portage was supposed to be, but could find no sign of it. We broke out flashlights and slowly patrolled the shoreline, craning our necks and straining our eyes. Portages in the BWCA can be difficult to find in broad daylight; anyone who has lost an afternoon searching for the way out of a deceptively formed lake like, say, Oyster, can fully appreciate the madness we were into here.

We "beached" the canoe (a charming BWCA euphemism for dragging it up over jagged ledge rock) and combed the shore on foot. After a half hour or so, we stumbled across the trail. The map said it was a 65-rod trek into Rifle Lake (a rod equals 16.5 feet). Mick fired up a Coleman lantern. With a lukewarm imitation of merry derring-do, we plunged into the woods with our gear, slipping on wet rocks and trudging through ankle-deep mud. In the harsh, inadequate lantern light, it all took on a surrealistic faintness, and the left hemisphere of my brain (the seat of rationality), not wishing to be associated with such insanity, began to pose questions like "What am I doing here?"

At last we made it to Rifle Lake, loaded the canoe, and shoved off into total blackness. Rifle Lake is long, narrow, and islandless; we figured it would be relatively easy to find the 170-rod portage that would take us into Bridge Lake, where our partners had said they would camp. Mist shrouded Rifle Lake; flashlights were almost useless. But so intense was our desire to reach camp that night that we pushed on slowly through the darkness, fervently hoping we wouldn't ram a rock and flip the canoe into the freezing water.

On the face of it, we were being stupid. On the other hand, it *was* an adventure. It was your typical wilderness risk: if you make it you're a hero; if you don't, you're an idiot. Had we capsized and drowned, paralyzed by the frigid autumn water, our names would have deservedly become synonyms for asininity. But we made it, and people shake their heads in grudging admiration of our pluck and perseverence. Don't they?

The 170-rod portage was foul and nasty at that hour of the night, and at Bridge Lake we dropped, exhausted, onto the rocks.

The main thing, however, was that despite the rugged trail, made doubly hazardous by the darkness, Mick and I were both reasonably intact.

"Mick," I said, "we used up a lot of brownie points tonight. If I were you, I'd be real careful for the next five years or so. You know, stay away from ladders, deep water, sharp objects."

We slipped into Bridge Lake at about 10:30 and started singing loudly to attract our companions' attention. Feeling voyageuristic, we thought it appropriate to do a few numbers in French. Sure enough, after a few minutes of our demented caroling, a campfire blazed into life ahead and to our right. Laughing triumphantly, we paddled into camp; reveling in our fellow adventurers' expressions of disbelief, we pigged out on trail food, clumsily pitched a tent, and gratefully hit the sack.

We were back in the canoes before sunrise, gliding silently across Bridge Lake through early morning fog, heading upstream on a small river that empties into the lake. We came upon a beaver dam not far from the mouth and pulled our canoes over it as quietly as possible. A little farther upstream, the river widens into a large pool—quintessential moose habitat. We drifted to a stop and waited, and fidgeted with Opening Day eagerness.

The morning was ghostly, utterly still. In the gradually brightening eastern sky, Mars and Venus glittered coldly in the constellation of Leo. What portents were these? A beaver surfaced, wrinkling the water. We heard him take a breath and watched him swim across our prows, lily pads bobbing gently in his wake. He was well past us before he folded his body for a violent, tail-slapping dive that echoed like the crack of a whip. In a few moments, the first rays of the rising sun backlit the fog and the somber grays of water and forest were suffused with delicate pastels. I was glad we didn't see a moose there; gunshots would have been absurdly out of place.

After waiting in ambush for a time, scanning the shoreline through telescopic sights, we decided to split up. Mick and I would paddle upstream to the source of the river, a small lake called Delta. Mike and Gerry would hang around the pool.

The river exits Delta Lake by means of a short stretch of white water. A 40-rod portage links Delta and the river's calm water. Rod for rod, that portage is one of the most treacherous I've ever seen, its most prominent feature being a steep, rocky hill that borders an almost vertical 20-foot drop to the rapids.

"How'd you like to haul a moose carcass across this one?" I said. Mick and I laughed wickedly as we considered the masochistic possibilities.

We spent the rest of the day cruising the woods and floating along shorelines in the general area of Delta and Bridge Lakes. The four of us convened for brief strategy meetings throughout the day, then split up again to cover as much territory as possible. We tried to stay close enough together that we would all hear any rifle shot.

Around 3 P.M., Mike saw a cow at a distance in heavy brush. He held his fire. We'd resolved to hold out for a large bull, at least for the first day or two. For Mick and me, the highlight of the afternoon was a nap on some warm rocks. The day had blossomed into the seductive Indian-summer variety, and for more than an hour we dozed in the sun like a couple of old dogs. Any passing moose (and no doubt there was one) must have been much amused.

After our languid siesta, we made one more lazy pass through a secluded bay. It smelled of bass, and we lusted after the fishing gear we'd neglected to bring. In the midst of a bittersweet discussion about how well some fresh fish would please the palate, we thought we heard four or five shots. We listened attentively and decided they had come from back on Lake Two—some other party hitting paydirt. As the sun descended toward the western horizon, we paddled back to camp, planning how we would clean out our partners in a friendly game of Smear. They were still out in the woods, so Mick and I started preparing supper. We didn't finish.

At sundown we spied a canoe coming down the lake with

only Mike aboard. The shots we'd heard had been our companions'. There was work to be done. Before Mike reached shore, we had hastily assembled our dressing-out tools: a one-ton cable hoist, eight cheesecloth meat sacks, a plastic tarp, towels, a saw, and the lantern. We launched the extra canoe that Mike and Gerry had towed in; with each of us in a canoe, we started stroking madly back toward Delta Lake. Mike filled us in on the way.

He and Gerry had walked over that brutal 40-rod portage. There they'd seen a large cow on the shore about 350 yards across Delta. There had been a minimum of discussion. Both had taken aim through telescopic sights; on the count of three, each had fired three shots. The moose had never flinched. She'd ambled along for a hundred more feet, wobbled a little, and then fallen, knocking down a balsam tree with a four-inch trunk.

"I thought," said Mick archly, "that we were waiting for a bull?"

Mike just shrugged and gave us a silly grin. Enough said. Meat was meat, and to hell with antlers. They were too heavy anyway.

As we rammed the beaver dam and leaped out to drag the canoes over it, darkness was already falling. There was a moon, but it was a thin crescent already low in the west. The night was destined to be clear and starlit, but very dark. And cold. The dusk had a frosty edge to it, promising temperatures in the 20s by morning.

We left two canoes at the start of the portage and lugged the third over with the butchering gear. By the time we'd crossed Delta to where Gerry sat by the fallen moose, it was fully night. Mick lit the lantern. In its stark, eerie light, I saw the cow for the first time—she was lying on her side, and her belly looked to be about four feet high. The sight staggered me. What in the world were we going to do with this? It was a black night in the wilderness, and we were a lake, a portage, a river, a beaver dam, and half of another lake away from camp. Camp was four lakes and four portages away from our trucks.

Mike was calmer. He coolly regarded our moose as just another engineering problem. The first obstacle was the unfortunate balsam, which prevented our rolling the carcass onto its back. Reaching under the moose with the small buck saw, Mike laboriously cut through the tree while the rest of us hefted the dead weight of the cow out of his way as best we could. Then, with the tree removed, each of us grabbed a leg and, with straining muscles and visceral grunts, managed to turn our prey onto her back.

While I held the lantern and steadied the carcass, the other three unsheathed knives and got down to business. We'd be carrying the beast out on our backs, so she would have to be skinned and quartered on the spot—not only to make (barely) manageable loads but also to start the meat cooling as rapidly as possible. The cold weather was a blessing in one way: we didn't have to worry about flies.

As the hide came off, I was amazed by how much heat and steam the carcass generated. Soon we were all shedding jackets and rolling up sleeves. There was a strong odor and lots of gore, but we were caught up in a kind of primal exaltation. Ancient predatory juices were flowing. Mick was displaying a surprising virtuosity with his skinning knife. Gerry, the old veteran, was impressed.

"You're pretty good at this," he said. At that moment I figured the blade would surely slip and lop off one of Mick's fingers. (As it turned out, it wasn't until two weeks later—in the comfort and relative safety of his own kitchen, under bright fluorescent lights, carving up a harmless squash—that Mick cut his thumb clean to the bone. I reminded him then that I'd warned him about his dangerously waning supply of brownie points.)

It was arduous work, all the harder because we were racing against time. There was only so much fuel in the lantern, and our flashlights would be inadequate for the job. Mick estimated we had three and a half to four hours of light to work with. After about two hours, we finally entered the chest cavity.

"Look at this," Mike said. He held up a mushroomed bullet.

It had done its lethal, high-powered work on the body tissues of the moose, but had spent its energy before it could produce an exit wound. In the light of the lantern, the bullet glistened like a precious gem unexpectedly uncovered. Yet there is no more deadly shape in the world. "Is it mine or yours?" Mike asked.

Gerry inspected it for a moment, then softly replied, "She was a majestic animal. We shouldn't have shot her. She was much prettier alive."

Here was a man who'd waited twelve years for this moment. Could he really be regretting it? He'd been enjoying the trip immensely, but now he seemed subdued. The sight of the fatal bullet had made an impression on all of us. What a contrast there was between the hard, unforgiving metal and the soft, once-vibrant organs of the moose. What chance had she had against a .30-06 with a scope? But that wasn't the point, was it? It was the hunt, not the kill, that mattered. Gerry wasn't sorry he'd hunted, only that he'd killed. The anticipation overshadowed the outcome, and he was caught upon the horns of an ancient dilemma: when dreams come true they are no longer dreams, and men must live by dreams. A part of Gerry had died with that moose.

Perhaps it was more complex than that. Were we worthy of this animal? Could *we* proudly roam the wilderness at will, in sun or snow, through forest or muskeg, living off the land and keeping the wolf packs at bay? We'd come to the moose's turf, but we'd ignored the house rules. Not with fangs or claws had we brought her down. We hadn't scrambled on all fours through the cruel brush, our noses twitching with the scent of her spoor. We hadn't chased her, lungs near bursting, only to face her flaring nostrils and massive, slashing hooves. We'd made no desperate leaps at her flanks to rip and tear her flesh with our own teeth. We'd come from another world and brought our own rules. It was as if we'd challenged the Minnesota Vikings to a football game, and then showed up with .357 magnums instead of shoulder pads. Our encounter with the Delta Lake moose was an unequal contest, and it had cost the magnificent moose her life. No, we were not worthy of her. Nor was our remorse anything new or unique; hunters from the Ojibway on down have known it. "The wolf and the caribou are one," according to an Indian proverb, but we, predators from another world, are outsiders, invaders. Unlike our ancestors, we don't even need the meat. We can't justify the hunt; we can only enjoy it. We need the quest and not the kill, but the way of the world is that you can't have one without the other. The best we could do was to make damn sure we didn't waste the meat. In this, at least, we were determined to be worthy.

It was close to midnight when we finished the bloody deed. The meat, in eight large chunks that weighed between seventy-five and one hundred pounds each, filled all of our bags. The hide, well over a hundred pounds by itself, was rolled into a bundle. Just as we started to stumble through the brush, staggering under the weight of the meat, the lantern sputtered and died. Mike and I ferried the first load of meat and gear back across Delta, and I began hauling it over that harrowing portage while he went back for more. With a flashlight in one hand and the mouth of a sack gripped tightly in the other, I struggled beneath the pungent bag of muscle. A heavy frost had descended on the trail; negotiating it was like trying to climb a very rough and steep skating rink. It was cold, but we were all sweating like pack mules. We'd had little food or water in the last several hours. At the river end of the portage, I lay on the shore and took a half-dozen gulps of water, and the others did the same.

When I'd made two precarious runs over the portage, Mike and Mick arrived with another load of meat. Mick joined me as a beast of burden. Mike and Gerry soon delivered the last of the loads from the far side of Delta, and all four of us grappled with those merciless forty rods. The owls must have been amazed at the strange procession of bobbing flashlights, cursing humans, and bloody sacks.

My canoe was filled first. I shoved off into the river alone, heading downstream toward Bridge Lake. The water and the banks were engulfed in blackness. I navigated by the sky. The treetops alongside the narrow river framed a star-studded expanse, and by looking into the middle distance I could work my way downriver. The October night was breathtakingly clear. Constellations were brilliant and vivid. They seemed to be not light-years away but hanging just out of reach. I traced the Little Dipper to Polaris, visually measuring the distance from the horizon to the Pole Star. This was indeed a northern night. There wasn't the slightest hint of movement in the air, not so much as a ripple on the water. The only sound was the soft rush of current past the keel of my canoe and the muted gurgling of my paddle. I worked as silently as I could; it seemed the courteous and reverent thing to do.

The unearthly stillness was shattered when I entered the wide spot in the river where we'd paused that morning. A startled beaver slapped its tail not ten feet from the canoe, and I nearly fell out. I laughed aloud. I could hear water rushing over the dam long before I saw its dim outline, and that helped. It was easy to charge over it with an empty canoe in daylight, but now I was carrying a couple hundred pounds of meat and was as good as blind. I got up as much speed as I could, but the prow of the canoe just barely rode up onto the dam. I had to climb gingerly over three sacks of meat to reach the prow and then step out on top of the dam. The shock of the freezing water only added to the exhilaration of the night. With some difficulty, I tugged and yanked at the canoe until I could push it over the dam and into the open water beyond. There wasn't far to go now. I paddled cheerfully down the rest of the river, bumping into a rock or two.

I rounded the last point before our campsite, and the dark expanse of Bridge Lake opened up before me. I gasped at the site. Mighty Orion, the hunter, ruler of the winter skies, was just rising in glory above the eastern horizon. To the north, the aurora borealis madly danced. The ethereal green rays vibrated, rushing across the sky in curtains of light and silhouetting the tops of the spruce. I felt as if I were in a fairyland, transported whole into some ancient Norse saga.

Yet as I neared the campsite, I began to feel the effects of the past twenty-four hours. Sleep had played a minor role, and I was being overtaken by that wonderful weariness you can know only in the bush. I expended my last reserves of energy to kindle a fire and put some supper on the grill. I had no flashlight, so I grubbed around on hands and knees in the dark to gather kindling and wood. I wanted to have a hot meal ready for the rest of the crew; it was a matter of hubris. The first tentative flames felt as good as anything in recent memory, and the taste of hot food was simply indescribable.

When the others arrived, we spent an hour eating, drying our feet, and salting down the moose hide. Stretched out, it covered about fifty square feet. With food in our bellies we turned a little cocky, and there was some crazy talk of breaking camp and pushing on. After all, it was close to 2 A.M.; daylight was only four hours away. For once, common sense prevailed. We crawled into our tents for a short rest. That this was a wise move was irrefutably proven by Mick, who, as he and I settled into our sleeping bags, pulled out a Snickers bar, gave me half, stuffed the other half in his mouth, and lay back to get comfortable. In the morning, he discovered the candy still in his mouth. That's tired.

Dawn brought another mist-shrouded morning. We inhaled some oatmeal, broke camp, and headed out of Bridge Lake. Mick and I each took a canoe-load of meat, and Mike and Gerry piled the gear in their craft. We met several other parties on the way out, all of them skunked so far. (We had to remind ourselves it was only the second day of the season.) They cast envious eyes at our grisly cargo, like something out of a Hitchcock movie—bloodstained bags, bloodstained canoes, bloodstained hands.

We arrived at the Lake One landing before noon and loaded

Mike's truck half full of meat and hide—about seven hundred pounds in all. Before we shoved off for Ely in search of beer, I cast a final glance at the lake and thought of dreams come true and left behind. This was one for the grandchildren, all right. An incident on the way out had summed it up. On our second-to-last portage that morning, we'd met a party going the other way, and they asked us where we'd bagged the moose.

"Well," I replied, "just head up to Delta Lake. There's some mean portaging and some long paddling, but there's moose up there. Where've you guys been hunting?"

In an apologetic tone one member of their group said, "Oh, just around Lake One and Two here. But," he quickly added, "I wanted to do what you guys did—just put our heads down and push into the woods, but . . ." and he trailed off and shrugged.

"Well, good luck," I replied, and hurried on over the portage so he could save face. I was reminded of a quote from writer-adventurer Bil Gilbert: "Those who stop where reason and instinct command never reach the best and highest places of all."

Mick and I had been to another of those places the previous spring. We went for an extended stroll in the woods and encountered some wondrous manifestations. For example, near the middle of a beaver dam we found a dollar bill. We couldn't imagine why it hadn't long since been swept away. Perhaps it had just arrived—a possibility as improbable as its perch, for it was early May and we were seven miles down the Kekekabic Trail. When people use the word "wilderness," where we were is what they mean. The mysterious greenback was not the only surprise the cruel Kekekabic would spring on us—just the only harmless one.

The Kekekabic Trail meanders for forty-two miles through the heart of Minnesota's BWCA, from the Fernberg Road east of Ely to the Gunflint Trail north of Grand Marais. The notion of hiking the Kek had been in my mind for years, fueled by survivors' wild-eyed tales of the perils it threatened—and promised. The boss of a federal trail crew in the 1940s wrote: "The Kekekabic Trail is one of the toughest, meanest rabbit tracks in North America." James W. Buchanan writes, in his *Minnesota Walk Book:* "An experienced backpacker that I talked with—one who had hiked on both the Appalachian and the Pacific Crest Trails—told me that while hiking the Kekekabic, his feet became so sore and badly blistered that he developed a case of blood poisoning—in spite of heavy hiking boots." Sam Cook, an outdoors writer for *The Duluth News-Tribune & Herald,* attempted the Kek in 1982; his party turned back, defeated. Cook's report on the trip made the Kek seem a thing possessed—a malevolent spirit bent on crushing human bodies and minds.

The verdict was unanimous, and the idea of taking on the Kek became a seductive, enchanting desire. Well-worn paths, abundant signs, and detailed maps all have their place, but Mick and I were after a different sort of jaunt. We wanted to feel like Lewis and Clark, not like Boy Scouts from Chicago. They could go to Isle Royale.

The Kek is no longer an official Forest Service Trail. In fact, the Service discourages its use. We learned that sobering, captivating tidbit when we ran over to a local printer to pick up some topographic maps of the BWCA. The clerk at the counter told us the Forest Service wanted to wipe the Kek off the most recent maps. The printer would have none of such cartographic censorship. (As it turns out, the moon is better mapped than the Kek. Ours may be the age of the vanished frontier, but the Kekekabic Trail remains, if not quite uncharted territory, at least *mis*charted. How refreshing.)

In *Minnesota Walk Book,* Buchanan warns that the Kek "is not a trail that can be walked in two or three days. Take at least four days, five are better." Well, that was a gauntlet thrown if ever I saw one. Mick and I vowed to conquer the Kek in three days. Two would be better.

On the sixth of May, we had ourselves dropped off at the trailhead near the end of the Fernberg Road. As the sound of the car faded away, I relished a momentary case of butterflies. We were on our own before the "toughest" and the "meanest." The sun had just set. We hiked in about half a mile and pitched our tent in the middle of trail. Near a little brook that drained a half-frozen swamp, with the stars winking through the naked, spindly branches of ash trees, we crouched beside the murmuring water and shared the excitement of confronting an unknown trail. Already we could see the path was not well traveled.

Mick lit a cigarette. Before he crushed it out, it was the only light in the woods. Having devoured two large pizzas in Ely (a ceremonial rite against the off chance that it would be our last civilized meal), we had no need of a cooking fire. In the frosty darkness we reviewed our strategy one last time. At dawn we would break camp. On the first day, while still fresh (and fueled by pizza), we'd push for as much distance as we could manage. If we could pound out twenty miles on Day One, surely we'd be able to reach the Gunflint in three days. From all reports, the first half would be the tougher; it would be best to tackle it while we were still "new." We bedded down early, brimming with confidence, sleeping contentedly on the Kek as if we belonged there—arrogance that would not go unpunished.

At six o'clock the next morning, we munched a quick breakfast and then pushed off at a brisk pace, heading into the rising sun. We soon discovered that the Kek consists of three basic materials: rocks, roots, and mud (and sometimes, in early May, snow and ice). Mud is merely unpleasant—extremely so when you sink past your ankles, as we often did. Rocks and roots are something else again. To sprain an ankle or twist a knee in your own back-yard is a trivial thing; to do so on the Kek is a matter of some seriousness. At the very best, you'll suffer. At the worst . . . well, suffice it to say that help is always far away. Even if you avoid sudden injury, you are at risk on the Kek from the simple wear and tear on joints and muscles unaccustomed to hiking an obstacle course. In many places the Kek merely follows, like water, the path of least resistance. We often found ourselves hopping from boulder to boulder in dry streambeds, an inherently ridiculous proposition when strapped into a backpack. At other times we picked our way across the tops of beaver dams; on the Kek there are none of those split-log footbridges that the paternalistic Forest Service is so fond of erecting over swamps and mudholes. The Kek just ends at the dams, so we used the beavers' handiwork as bridges, with balancing poles to aid our crossings. It was gratifyingly tough. This was the sort of jaunt we were after.

As might be expected of an unmaintained trail, deadfalls litter the Kek. Out of morbid curiosity, I counted them as we hiked. Before we were finished, we struggled around, over, under, and through 1,286 dead trees—some of them crisscrossed in such evil jumbles of branches and spikes that the "easiest" way to get by was to crawl underneath on hands and knees, and sometimes bellies. They were more than an inconvenience, because they sapped our energy far more quickly than mere hiking.

Despite it all, we believed we were making good time. The trail was faint, but easier to follow than we'd expected. Some of the old trail markers—small blue plastic diamonds nailed to trees—still hung as guideposts, but our chief scout was moose dung. You couldn't walk a half dozen paces without stumbling upon a pile of pellets. Moose traffic, it seemed, was the only thing keeping the Kek open.

We lost the trail, for the first time, at around 9:30. We came to a pond surrounded by swamp; the trail just ended. Our map informed us that the Kek headed northeast across the swamp. A line of rotting logs, half sunken in the muskeg, apparently led on to high ground. Gingerly hopping from log to log like neophyte burlers, foolishly expending energy in a vain attempt to keep our feet dry, we reached the high ground with waterlogged boots and no sign of a trail. We dropped our packs, circled back and forth through the brush for close to half an hour, and found not the slightest hint of a path. The moose scat formed no pattern.

There was nothing to do but backtrack across the swamp and pick up the trail where we were last sure of it. After several more minutes of searching, we finally found our way. The map had lied to us. The trail turned southeast, sidestepping the swamp.

We proceeded, a bit shaken, in anxious search of some definite landmark. We soon came to a lake with a small island in the middle. Our map said that a lake called Becoosin had a small island in the middle. We felt better—troubled only by the fact that we stood to the south of the lake. According to the map, the Kek goes to the north of Becoosin. A high wooded ridge was visible in the distance. Our compass told us it stood to the northeast, and so did the map—which informed us, ominously, that our landmark was called Disappointment Mountain. It was prominent enough to serve as our guide for the next several miles—when we could see it, that is.

The Kek is not a scenic trail. Most of the time we were marching through deep forest. "Wilderness" does not fully convey the quality of the terrain. "Primeval" gives a better sense of it. We knew that others had trod these woods before us, but it wasn't difficult to imagine otherwise. I've spent a lot of time in the bush, from Isle Royale to the Rockies, but there on the Kek I felt, for the first time, "in the woods"—where losing your way is no temporary annoyance but a flirtation with death.

We lustily flirted with that fate—about three times an hour. We'd be hiking along, enjoying the slightly altered state of consciousness that accompanies sustained and strenuous activity, when suddenly we'd stop short, realizing with a start that the trail had vanished. Sometimes all it took was a bit of looking around, but often we had to drop our packs and mount a full-scale search to both sides of our line of travel.

About noon, we stopped for lunch on the shore of Moiyaka Lake—basking in the sunshine, satisfied in the suspicion that we'd made a dozen miles since daybreak. After a spartan, rodent-style meal of nuts, dried fruit, and granola bars, we hoisted our packs to push off. Mick bent over the water to fill his canteen. He felt a twinge in his gut, but paid it little mind. A mile or so down the trail, he realized that something was terribly, painfully wrong. The Kek had hit him below the belt. With some trepidation, Mick dropped his pants to take a look. He is exaggerating only slightly when he says his testicles were swollen up "like tennis balls."

"You might have a hernia," I said. "You want to turn back?"

Mick hesitated, ruefully buckling his belt. "It's not normally an immediately serious problem," I said. "But out here . . . and if it's too painful . . ."

"No," he said. "Let's do it."

"Are you sure?"

"Yes."

Mick insisted he could handle the pain. Walking twenty-nine miles forward seemed less burdensome than walking thirteen miles back. We pushed on. This was the sort of jaunt we were after.

The day was bright with spring sunshine. The temperature hovered in the 40s. We were drenched in sweat. Low, mushy terrain had given way to gigantic granite ridges as we'd approached Kekekabic Lake—repeatedly climbing from 1500 feet to 1800 feet and back down, seesawing over rocky trails so steep that they forced us to become four-legged creatures. Arduous, exhausting work. As the miles slipped behind us, Mick's special pain abated somewhat—probably, I kidded, because everything else hurt so much.

All of our aches temporarily vanished when we came across two stupendous white pines growing on the side of a ridge. We caught our breath, awestruck. Here was genuine virgin timber— close to a hundred feet tall, several hundred years old. We had to bend over backwards, craning our necks, just to catch a glimpse of their tops. Mick and I joined hands and hugged those magnificent trunks; our twelve-foot armspan didn't come close to completing the embrace. These were the sort of giants that covered northern Minnesota and Wisconsin before the arrival of the white man—an amazing thought, but not nearly so incredible as the fact that those monstrous pines were logged off in less than a century, with hand tools and horses. No wonder men believed they'd never deplete the forest. But they did, and even the meanness of the Kek couldn't stop them. We found an old band-saw blade beside the trail. It lay in a rusty tangle, slowly merging with the forest floor. It must have weighed well over a hundred pounds. My heart quailed at the thought of packing it into the wilderness. What sort of men had such endurance, such determination? Our exertions seemed suddenly tarnished—timid, lackluster.

Hiking the Kek is like running behind a bad offensive line. You pay the price for every yard you gain—stepping between rocks, tripping over roots, clambering over deadfalls, slipping in the mud. At mid-afternoon we began to think about a campsite. We needed to camp near water, but we were then negotiating the crest of a long, high ridge to the south of Kekekabic Lake. Aside from stagnant puddles, there would be no easily accessible water until we reached Harness Lake, which appeared to be three or four miles off. We thought we'd covered close to twenty miles; in any case, Mick couldn't go much farther. We decided to crash at the next stream or pothole.

The miles stretched on; no break in the dense forest. Mick's speech was becoming slurred, and he was stumbling more than usual. I was afraid he was becoming hypothermic. The conditions were ideal: heavy exertion in cool weather. Our canteens were empty.

"We've got to stop," Mick mumbled. "I can't go much farther."

He couldn't even hold his head up anymore. But we had to push on to water. I urged him to hang on.

At about 4:30, we came upon a cracked and weatherbeaten sign nailed to a tree: "Fernberg Road, 27 miles." An arrow pointed in the direction we'd come from. It was as if the scraggly sign had spoken aloud. Twenty-seven miles! It didn't seem possible. Small wonder we were exhausted. Through drooping eyes Mick peered at the sign and swore—whether in triumph or remorse, I couldn't tell. He looked terrible.

Around the next bend in the trail, we surprised a large cow moose. Her coat had the thin and ragged look of springtime. She gave us a baleful glance and lumbered off into the trees. We were equally unimpressed, so focused were we upon our own misery. Only one sight could excite us—and thankfully, around five o'clock, we finally saw it. Water. A lake. Harness Lake. No sojourner in the desert ever looked upon a more inviting oasis.

We trudged to the shore. Mick collapsed. He wormed out of his pack and curled up in a fetal position. I filled our canteens, and we both slurped and chugged as much as we could. I hurriedly started a fire and prepared a pot of soup and rice. We were famished, and as the sun neared the horizon, cold.

Mick came around in about twenty minutes. With some rest, some water, a fire for soggy feet, and the realization of what we'd done, his eyes became alert, his speech crisp. We laughed. We shouted. We were exultant. Twenty-eight miles on the Kek. In one day! Twenty-eight miles of wicked, torturous wilderness trail. Mick was aglow. He'd never before pushed himself to the utter limit of physical and psychological endurance. He'd been tried and acquitted, and through his body coursed the powerful drugs released by supreme effort and numbing pain.

"I never dreamed of doing anything like this," he said. Then he laughed again, intoxicated on the wine of triumph. "No one's going to believe us," he said. This was precisely the sort of jaunt we were after.

Supper, we swore, was the best meal we'd ever had. We pitched the tent, gathered firewood, and settled down by the fire to enjoy a little tobacco and the antics of two beavers swimming around on the lake.

"You know, Mick," I said contentedly, tapping my snuff box, "you were close to real trouble back there."

"I know," he said, his grave tone giving way to an impish grin. "So were you."

Mick revealed that as he'd pushed on and on under my insistent lash, he'd grown angry. Disoriented and hypothermic, he'd started looking for a loose rock on the trail. "I was going to bash your head in," he said. His plan: to gobble down all our food, then crawl into the bush and die. He was serious. He'd been closer to the edge than I'd realized. I told him that next time I'd remember to pack a pistol. He assured me there wouldn't be a next time.

As twilight faded into impenetrable darkness, the temperature dropped rapidly. We had little doubt it would be freezing by morning—probably in the teens. Before seeking refuge in our sleeping bags, we hoisted our packs into the air. We'd noticed bear sign about, and the thought of losing our provisions was a sobering thought. Satisfied with our arrangements, we crawled into the tent and passed out.

We hit the trail the next morning at 6:30, and punched out onto the Gunflint Trail at 2 P.M. We'd hiked the Kek in a day and a half. The last fourteen miles were a bit less rugged than the first twenty-eight (which isn't saying much), and the second day was something of an anticlimax. There was that one spot, though, a little west of Agamok Lake, where the Kek climbed to the crest of a bare ridge that at last offered us an unobstructed view of the Boundary Waters wilderness: a vast, majestic panorama of unbroken forest. Undulating ridges, bristling with trees, dwindled away to the horizon on every side—a sight at once humbling and magnifying. We were tiny indeed before the sheer breadth and presence of that wild, sprawling land—two small living things among a billion living things. But we had *walked* that land. For a moment we were its masters.

And Mick was right. No one has ever believed us. Perhaps his grandchildren will.

EIGHT
Telling Tales

The narrow road is impassable, the spring runoff rendering it soft and pulpy. Rastus has buttressed the worst spot with aspen logs, laying down a crude section of corduroy road over a mudhole. It looks like a forsaken stretch of the Burma Road. In reality it's his driveway, over a quarter mile through the woods and across a field.

Long, and often regrettable, experience with local "driveways" convinces us we should hike in. Sooch figures his four-wheel-drive pickup could barrel through, but not without generating an ugly set of ruts. That is taboo. Backwoods etiquette demands that you treat a muddy two-track driveway with deference.

As we approach the house on foot, dodging little clusters of goat droppings, the voice of a piano filters through the unfinished fiberboard walls. Sounds like Mozart; we've caught Rastus at the keyboard. Sooch bangs on the side of the house, bellowing a loud monosyllable of greeting, like a buck snorting in a thicket.

As have many of the people of Side Lake, Rastus is building his own house, and like many, it's not finished and perhaps never will be. Once you're to the point where snow and mosquitoes can't get in, it's easy to lose interest. Of course it's also easy to run out of money, as Rastus well knows.

Without waiting for a formal response, Sooch, his girlfriend, Sue, and I hop up the loose concrete blocks that serve as outside steps and enter the house. Rastus is living in a semi-completed room on the second floor, and we ascend a treacherous circular staircase, Sooch yelling over the piano. The music abruptly ceases as Rastus finally hears us coming. He's a private pianist, loath to give recitals. He claims he's no good, but we can hear that he's lying. He greets us at the top of the stairs, delighted to have company.

His one insulated space is kitchen, bedroom, and living room all in one. The "bathroom" is outside; the kitchen sink drains into a bucket. It's a cluttered and cozy study in contrasts. An antique enameled gas stove, ancient but functional, is offset by a high-quality, high-tech stereo system. On one wall is a faded tapestry, a scene from the Old World, frilly and baroque. Opposite is a soiled American flag with forty-eight stars. There's his piano, with a metronome and stacks of classical sheet music; in the corner are a rifle, a chain saw, and a hockey stick.

Rastus is a chef—not a cook, but an excellent chef. Sometimes people pay him for it, otherwise it's the sawmill. He's a city boy born and bred, thirty-six years old, and along with Filmore, his conceited cat, living alone in the woods. What's he doing here? He says he heard it was nice country. That was ten years ago.

We all settle in and Rastus brews some herbal tea. Soon we are contentedly sipping away, like mandarins or flower children. We look as if we're posing for the cover of the *Mother Earth News,* and Sooch shakes his head and laughs.

"In the old days," he says, "we would have stumbled up those stairs with a case of beer and a bottle of whiskey. Now look at this? Stinking tea!"

The rest of us grin as mention of "the old days" (Sooch is all of thirty-nine, a remarkable total, considering) reminds him of several good stories at once. He has another spot of tea and picks one out of his fervid brain:

The Marines were under attack. The crashing and roaring of incoming rockets and mortar rounds rolled across the base like a violent storm. At the first shriek of danger everyone had scrambled into bunkers or vaulted into trenches. All were feeling naked and vulnerable beneath the barrage—all but one. Standing on *top* of a bunker in the wide-open, shrapnel-torn air, a young Marine defied the Vietnamese assault. He wore no helmet and brandished no weapon. Instead, he ripped open his shirt, and baring his chest to the sky, he screamed obscenities at God and the Virgin Mary, daring them to kill him. They didn't. Below him, inside the bunker, other Marines had more reverent, if no less fervent, conversations with the Deity. One of them was Sooch.

I wasn't there, but as Sooch tells the story, in his graphic, vulgar, and unforgettable way, I feel as if I've experienced it. He has a way with words. But it's also in his eyes. They take on a sheen, a particular luster. As they focus on the middle distance you can seen that he's seeing it all again. His face is like a movie screen, projecting the scene in all its glorious insanity.

"The man was nuts," he says, "a real wacko!" But it's clear from the way he relishes the story, from the way he shakes his head as he remembers, that the crazy young Marine is not recalled without a certain amount of respect. There is honor in defiance, and Sooch displays esteem for the blasphemous rebel. People may hear it in my voice when I tell stories about Sooch.

Like the night the paramedics thought he was dead. Hell, they were sure he was dead; they radioed in and said so. The car, a girlfriend's, was demolished. Sooch had busted the windshield with his face and twisted the steering column out of shape with his body. He'd rear-ended a parked State Patrol squad car at about 55 mph, knocking it 36 feet, in gear. As it turned out, the unfortunate state trooper who was sitting inside would survive, though it would be several hours before he would know it. Contrary to appearances, Sooch would also live. In fact, he would escape from the hospital that very night, refusing to stay. But his life was changed; his attention had been caught. Instead of a two-by-four, he'd taken a four-door sedan right between the eyes. In short order he'd checked himself back into a hospital, this time for a thirty-day chemical dependency treatment program. That was six years ago, and he's been on the wagon ever since.

And so now we drink tea. It's lubrication enough for yarn-spinning tongues, and we trade stories in the backwoods shack, soothed by the isolation and savoring our sense of companionship. Rastus's goats remind Sooch of a brief career in livestock management. It seems he and a couple of buddies once bought a pig on a whim, and decided to get some pork chops and bacon out of the deal. Sooch phoned a butcher and asked him to do the honors.

"Is it a clean pig?" the man asked. Meaning was it white, or did its hide have patches of color?

Sooch, ignorant of the jargon of hog raisers, looked at his pig, caked with mud and fecal matter, and lied.

"Yeah, it's a clean pig," he replied.

When he hung up the phone he said to his buddies: "Boys, we got to wash this damn pig!"

So they hustled their porcine hostage into a car wash and started jamming quarters into the machines. They hosed and scrubbed and rinsed and wrestled, and six quarters later the black and white pig was immaculate. As a finishing touch, they gave it a wax job.

Justly proud of their "clean" pig, they brought it to the butcher. He took one look at the black patches on the hide and exclaimed, "I thought you said it was a clean pig."

Sooch was flabbergasted.

"Clean! Are you kidding? We put a buck fifty into washing this sucker!"

Sooch says that even after fifteen years, the butcher still loses it every time they meet. We howl with delight, and Sooch is on a roll. He's a collector of stories, and it's evident that telling them is one of the chief joys of his life. It helps him get through the winters, and by extension, it helps the rest of us as well. The vigor of his delivery is infectious, and many a backwoods shack has glowed in the presence of his well-turned tales.

Rastus fetches more tea, and Sooch spreads his arms to indicate the size of the hole he says his friend Maki once chopped in the ice. It was in early winter, and he'd fired up the sauna one last time before it got too cold. To honor tradition, he planned to dash from the hot sauna and plunge into the lake. The lake was already frozen over, but there was little more than an inch of ice, so it was easy to make a hole big enough to jump into.

After a long, sweltering stint in the 150-degree sauna, Maki burst out the door and ran naked through the snow to the edge of the lake. Pussyfooting it across the ice, he bravely plopped into the bone-chilling water, completely submerging himself for maximum effect. It was only about waist deep, and he came back up almost immediately, but instead of breaking the surface into the cold blue air, he bumped his head against solid ice. For a split second he was bewildered, and then raw fright set in. He'd lost the hole!

Maki was already alert. A quick dip in a freezing lake is a wonderful way to focus the mind. But it was the adrenaline that saved him. He knew he couldn't waste precious time looking for the hole; he could have drifted off in any direction, and the water was dark. So he crouched on the sandy bottom, bent at the knees, his legs tensed like two powerful springs, and his hands raised level with his head. Then, with the shocking energy of terror and desperation, he thrust himself violently upward against the ice sheet.

His buddies, who'd been watching from the sauna door, figured Maki was goofy to be lingering underwater for so long and were just beginning to worry when they saw him blast through the ice "like a big blue whale."

Freezing and frantic, gulping the beautiful air like a newborn babe (and what a slap on the butt), Maki bolted back into the sauna and cuddled up to the wood stove. As his teeth chattered, his body quivered, and his buddies laughed, he slowly began to thaw. Soon an acrid odor filled the sauna, and his companions, fearing the worst, pulled Maki away from the stove. Sure enough, his posterior was "smoldering."

Sooch winds up the story with an imitation of Maki's choreography when he realized he was now burned. These images of a man first frozen and then fried remind me of the time up on Lake Vermilion when three friends and I tried for a world record.

But it was not to Guinness that we appealed for recognition. We sought our fleeting glory through the good offices of the Finnish Embassy, for we were convinced we had stoked up the world's hottest sauna.

Thomas Edison, a celebrity of yesteryear, said that "genius is one percent inspiration and ninety-nine percent perspiration." In our case, inspiration preceded perspiration—and only a genius could have said beforehand whether they'd add up to 100 or 0. The inspiration came in the mail: an article in *Reader's Digest.* Lauding the benefits of saunas (pronounced sow-oo-na, since there are no diphthongs in Finnish), the writer mentioned in passing that the hottest sauna in Finland had reached 267 degrees Fahrenheit. That did sound a bit on the infernal side, but we were sure we could do better, or worse.

On a hot July day we stout-hearted men gathered at one of Minnesota's finest saunas. Built by loving Finnish hands, it was a tight, well-insulated, cedar-lined beauty. It was, in fact, an oven. We crammed the firebox of the stove with seasoned birch and, to demonstrate our sincerity, fired it up with a splash of gasoline. (Not recommended by any known consumer safety organization.) Newspaper and kindling simply did not promise the appropriate dramatic effect. In the time it takes gasoline to ignite, we had a mature blaze, and we kept it that way. No sooner was there space for another chunk of wood than it was duly stuffed in. This went on for hours.

As our little corner of Hell grew ever more hellish, we reviewed our strategy. We would shoot for 300 degrees. Achieving that, we'd write the Finnish Embassy to claim the world record. Then, to firmly establish our credibility, we'd commission T-shirts commemorating the event.

To gauge our progress, we'd placed an oven thermometer in the corner near the ceiling. We surpassed 250 degrees with surprising speed. In less than three hours of firing, we surpassed the 267-degree mark. The temperature was still rising, though more slowly. We decided that if we spent five minutes on the top bench at 300 degrees, any remotely sensible person, and even the Finns, would be satisfied.

There are, you see, three stations in a sauna. The top bench, where it's the hottest, is for Finns; the second bench is for Swedes; the floor is for everyone else. More than once over the years, I've seen this simple arrangement enforced in the service of ethnic pride. You'll be basking serenely in a sauna with four or five others when the Finnish blood in one of them begins to rise with the heat. Soon all the Slavs, Italians, Frenchmen, and other aliens are put on notice that a trial of fire is about to commence. With fanatical, xenophobic glee, the Finn pours water on the piping-hot rocks. A cloud of scorching, unbreathable steam, in wave upon deadly wave, rises from the stove and pummels everyone but the Finn to the deck or out the door—an exodus invariably accompanied by the giddy laughter of the parboiled perpetrator. Having finished off his inferior comrades, this Nordic devil is usually safe to sauna with for at least another year or so.

I didn't expect any outbreaks of chauvinistic madness in the world's hottest sauna. Although I was a Slav among three Finns, my colleagues had all seemed profoundly moved by how hot 267 degrees had felt when we made a short practice run at that temperature. No one had even thought of spilling any water, and there was even some talk about how maybe three minutes on the top bench might be sufficient to astonish the world.

After about four hours, the temperature reached 300 degrees. With wet washcloths over our faces, we entered the blast furnace. We'd already discovered that the air inside could not be inhaled unless it was filtered through moist fabric. The wooden bench was too hot to sit on without wetting it down. We should have had our hair wet as well, because we later noticed that it had been singed. We sat in tortured silence, staring at the 300-degree mark on the thermometer. No one wished to risk his watch (timepieces apparently being more precious than flesh and blood), so we counted off what we thought must be about four minutes, then bolted headlong out the door and onto the dock. It was only a half-dozen steps to the end, and then a short drop into seven feet of Lake Vermilion's 55-degree water.

I went numb instantly. Up from the rocky bottom I drifted, disembodied, floating in a womb-like world that was strangely lacking in sensation. The sudden contrast was so shocking to the biological system that it seemed as if nothing worked. For a moment all I could do was see, and that not very well. Surprisingly, no one drowned. With rubbery limbs and spongy brains, we all managed to struggle back onto the dock.

"I smell something burning," mumbled one of the Finns. We made a quick check of the sauna. Sure enough, some of the ceiling boards above the stove were starting to smolder. We damped the stove, doused the boards, and gloated over our survival of an ordeal that even dead wood could not endure.

The next day, I wrote to the Finnish Embassy in Washington, D.C., to claim the world record. They promptly replied with a booklet about saunas and a letter that made no mention of our record-breaking heroics. Probably because embassies are homes to diplomats, there was nothing in the reply that could be construed as certifiably insulting, but it was clear the Finns thought they were dealing with pranksters or idiots—maybe both.

We never had the T-shirts made, either, but we did carve our names and the pertinent data in the sauna door. The place has since been sold. I hope the new owners are suitably impressed by their curious artifact; I suppose they are merely baffled.

Though our achievement remains unrecognized, we rest secure in the knowledge that if anyone has topped 300 degrees, they've also burned down their sauna. There is comfort in that.

And in the fact that the stories flow on, one conjuring up another, heartening our existence. We are cheered and encouraged, hoping to live the stories which have not yet unfolded. A past implies a future, and we're comforted to know there are things to come.

Rastus brews another pot of tea.

NINE
Wide-Screen Window

We fought over the windows. Pam and I each held firm opinions about the design of the house, and the amount of glass to be used became a bone of contention.

Championing energy efficiency, I maintained that our windows should be few and small, sacrificing light for R-value. I preached, at length, about thermal transmittance.

"Don't be a pane," she replied, and then deflated the bravado of the energy crisis with one succinct but paradoxical argument: The winters are long, dark, and cold. Therefore we spend much more time indoors and we need large windows so we can enjoy the sight of the winter forest, letting in as much mood-altering sunshine as possible. After all, we were building in the midst of *scenery;* why block it out?

Well, they don't call them "picture windows" for nothing. Our big living room pane, roughly five by eight feet, is like a wide-screen TV. You can sit in front of that window and see it all: sex, violence, adventure, news, sports—and in color.

There's only one channel, and they don't change the stage set (we're always looking west), but it's a stirring backdrop. The forest starts about twenty-five feet from the glass, a mixed woods of young aspen and balsam dominated by a majestic white pine in the foreground, with coppices of mature birch in the background. We're very happy the white pine's been included. It's the only one on our entire forty acres, and there it is, placed right outside our wide-screen window (WW). Behind the trees is a small lake, perhaps two hundred yards distant, and after the leaves fall we catch brief, shimmering glimpses of it through swaying branches and boughs. But we always know it's there; that's the important thing.

The center of the action, the focus of most of the drama, is our bird feeder. Less than ten feet from the window, it's made out of redwood and glass and sits atop a length of one-inch galvanized pipe about five feet high. It serves the same purpose as the Carrington mansion on *Dynasty,* without, however, the ornate staircases. Here they opt for simple perches, an effective understatement.

Our favorite regulars, the beautiful personalities with flawed character, are the blue jays. They're pretty and they know it. In a world of camouflage and deception, of subtle mottled coats and earth tones, they're colored bright blue. It's made them skittish, and that's made them mean. All that quick glancing, darting, and dodging is exasperating, so they take it out on the little nuthatches and whoever else visits the feeder-mansion. Often there are three or four innocent and harmless black-capped chickadees pecking away at the sunflower seeds (wealth and power), and a blue jay will blow in and scatter them. The jay has plenty to consume on one side of the feeder but will maliciously hop around to the other perch, making sure there are no chickadees (hmph!) lowering the property values. The chickadees, the valiant little guys, common but courageous, fly right back to the opposite side of the feeder, brazenly refusing to be denied their share of the GNP. The greedy blue jays chase them off again, and so on, the high-speed action never slowing down. Every bird is a stunt bird.

Just when you're getting used to all the routine entrances and exits, the show takes an unexpected turn. One day, during the usually low-key mid-morning programming, a glittering lineup of guest stars dropped in. Forty-five evening grosbeaks inundated the set. They filled the aspens near the feeder, looking like yellow

Christmas tree ornaments gently bobbing in the breeze. There were so many they had to eat in shifts, some crowding the perches, others on the ground. A cast of dozens! And provocative. The males are bright yellow with distinctive, artistic markings on head, back, and wings. The females are muted, light yellow (almost lime), with a more uniform configuration, drab by comparison. So there you have it: *sex*. Vive la différence! It was tastefully done.

But forty-five or not, one vindictive blue jay ran them all off. He/she/it (jays are indistinguishable, not into explicit sex) grabbed at a few seeds, kicked a few out into the snow, then exited stage right, satisfied with a cameo appearance.

However, even the blue jays have their nemesis. The red squirrels are aliens, the equivalent of Godzilla, King Kong, or David Letterman. The last thing these dudes need is more food—they've been gathering pinecones and hazelnuts by the cheekful all summer and fall—but still they assault the feeder on a daily basis, wallowing in the seeds like fuzzy hogs. The jays stay away, either fearful or scandalized. I suspect they're racists—blue supremacists or something.

One of the biggest fans of WW is our cat, Bloody Alice. She's a professional killer, an expert assassin of rodents of all stripes, and the squirrels respect her. But she spends the bulk of the winter indoors, out of circulation—occasionally slaying the sofa, but mostly looking out the window. She likes to watch.

And like the rest of us she has her favorite programs. She's bored by the birds; the interminable antics of this long-running situation comedy have been known to lull her into ennui. She perks up when the squirrels come on, knowing a rodent when she sees one. But what really turns her crank are the mice. They adore a dramatic entry. They tunnel in from the woods like stealthy little snow-submarines—like the *Nautilus* under the North Pole—then *pop!* up through the crust at the base of the feeder. They hit the surface running, scrambling around for wayward seeds. This drives Alice crazy. She pastes her pink nose against the screen and cries—a long series of guttural meows, plaintive, angry, lustful.

I swear the mice know this, realizing she can't get at them, and that it deeply annoys her. How else to explain the mouse who one day faced the window, kicked back on tiny feet, and took a scornful little bow. (Or perhaps it was just choking on a bit of sunflower shell. Judge for yourself. I may have imagined it—you start seeing a lot of weird things by the end of the winter.)

Alice also gets a kick out of prime time. One night we saw her staring out into the pitch blackness, face near the glass and meowing appreciatively. We followed her gaze but could see nothing. I got a flashlight, aimed it at the dim form of the feeder, and flicked it on. Voilà. There was a flying squirrel on the perch, its big round black eyes staring into the light, unconcerned. Even as we watched a second squirrel, bat-like, ghostly, and fat, soared in and landed. The beam of light didn't bother it either. They both bothered Alice. It's what gets her through the winters.

We also see a news show on WW, but it's mostly a weather report. The forecasts are fairly accurate. When you see thunderheads rolling in from the northwest—upper right on the screen—you can figure it's going to rain. (Severe weather is the WW equivalent of the biblical blockbuster movie.) If you see clouds in December, it's going to snow. Which reminds me: that's the only kind of "snow" you see on our screen, and adjustments are unnecessary. Besides, I've never found any kind of knobs or dials. Routine maintenance is simple; a bottle of Windex and some paper towels are the only tools required.

However, the initial installation and alignment is critical. I mentioned our westerly view, and I highly recommend that channel. It's there you may enjoy that ever-popular and long-running series: sunsets (on almost daily). Naturally you have the option of picking up the eastern channel and catching sunrises, but they are scheduled at such inconvenient times. And since WW is not yet compatible with VCRs, you must watch all programming live.

If you're an amateur astronomer or a practicing pagan, you may fine-tune the installation of your WW so that on the equinoxes, the first day of spring (March 21) and the first day of autumn (September 21), the sun sets precisely in the center of your screen. It does that at our place. We can then track it north or south on a daily basis, depending upon the season, and we have a mini-Stonehenge, a natural calendar. It amazes our friends. Doesn't it?

Like most people, we watch a lot at night, and as many Americans do, we own two screens. Our second one is smaller and is attached (securely) to the front of our wood stove. We get only one channel on the stove too, but it's warm, colorful, and very efficient. I know we must sound like hopeless hedonists, but we enjoy watching both screens at the same time. First we turn on the small screen and let it warm up for a while. When all we can see is a red-orange bed of coals radiating a cozy, toe-snuggling glow, we turn out all the lights. We watch the soft, romantic illumination from the stove play along our log walls until our eyes are fully adjusted to the dimness. Then we look out our wide-screen window at the stars. For hours we watch as the summer constellations sink slowly into the west, the bright swath of the Milky Way leaving us for another season. Occasionally a meteor streaks in from outer space, leaving a fiery trail across the black sky. When we're really lucky, the northern lights appear, flashing in green or yellow waves, pulsating up to the zenith in scintillating rays and arcs. And maybe, after midnight, the last-quarter moon rises behind us and we see its cold white light shine through the icicles on the eaves, glittering like precious gems.

So who needs another channel?

But often it's necessary to leave the house, attracted by bright lights like fluttering moths. There is a smidgen of glitter in Side Lake: we live within five miles of two bars.

As a general rule, trees are many and people are few in northern

Minnesota. Entertainment extravaganzas are rare (aside from high-school hockey games); cultural events, as commonly defined, are almost nonexistent. But no matter how far into the bush you may be, a backwoods tavern is never too far away.

So what? No doubt such establishments *are* rustic, quaint, and possessed of a certain primitive charm, you say, but how much Canadian beer can one drink in a night? Ah, but you see, these remote and sleepy saloons are much more than mere watering holes. They are cultural centers in a very basic sense of the term.

What's your pleasure? Live music? Then back off and give old Eino Tumola some room at the bar. Eino's got to have space to play his fiddle—space, and liberal quantities of 7-Up. He's got to be tipsy to play, and 7-Up seems to do the trick. Eino, you see, was cultivating cannabis in the woods before a single hippie left the womb; he's still at it. He never brings the stuff to the bar, except in his bloodstream. The fiddle howls, Eino laughs, people clap, smile, and hoot: "Eino! Have another 7-Up!" Eino flashes a sly grin, eyes twinkling, sixty-year-old fingers flying.

Wanna dance? Then make some more room, because Ole Olson has emerged from the woods. Ole rides his bike eight miles to the bar, sometimes at night, in January if necessary—and Ole often finds it necessary. Around his neck hangs a leather pouch; in the pouch rests a small harmonica. When the ambience is right, Ole makes that harmonica wail and dances a spirited jig around the room, whirling and stomping his feet. One of Ole's favorite recreations is to approach an unsuspecting woman, finger the pouch around his neck, and ask, "Would you like to see my organ?" Somehow no one ever takes offense. Ole throws back his head and roars, sending a ripple of laughter the length of the bar.

Perhaps your tastes run along more cerebral lines. Then be attentive, because tavern talk runs hot and heavy on Saturday night. No subject is taboo; even thorny and perdurable quandaries are hashed and thrashed with gusto. One night someone asked, "Why do people have to die?" The query was addressed to no one in particular, so everyone gave it a shot. The discussion roiled and boiled, ranging far and wide and vagrantly across the landscape of human thought. It went on for more than an hour, with no one holding back. No one, that is, except Bobby, down at the far end of the bar. Bobby had been drinking quietly for eleven hours and now was staring into the limpid depths of yet another brandy and water.

"Hey, Bobby!" someone called out. "What do you think about this?"

Bobby slowly raised his head, his eyes peering with solemnity into profound distances. With the gravity of a sage, he replied: "He who shall, so shall he who." Further discussion seemed unnecessary.

Social issues your bag? Then you could do worse than talk to Lurch on a Saturday night. He'll be coming off a hard week of logging. You might bring up unionism and labor relations; Lurch's credentials are impeccable. It seems that Lurch used to run a skidder for Logger A. Logger B approached Logger A and offered to buy the skidder. Logger A agreed, and a deal was struck. But Lurch wouldn't get off the skidder. "If the skidder goes, then so do I," he said with finality. Logger B had no choice. He had to hire Lurch. A one-man union. The Teamsters should have such clout.

If you aren't easily amused—if your entertainment needs spill over into more esoteric regions—then you should have been around the night Terry tested his snowshoes. He'd just hand-crafted a beautiful pair of shoes, and he brought them to the tavern to show them off.

"What're they made of?" he was asked.

"The finest ash," he replied.

"Are they strong?"

With a condescending chuckle, Terry laid one of his shoes across two bar stools, climbed up onto the snowshoe bridge, and bounced his two-hundred-pound frame up and down. I know what you're thinking, and it *would* make a better story . . . but the snowshoe held. There was warm and general applause. If that level of excitement doesn't stir your soul, perhaps you'd be best off avoiding backwoods taverns.

But avoid them at your peril. There aren't all that many places to meet the likes of Rockford, or to see the likes of Rockford's bartop show. Rockford is a full-grown male raccoon with a weakness for Beer Nuts. He industriously washes his Beer Nuts in a saucer of beer, then eats the nuts, then drinks the beer. After several servings, he'll lie on his back on the floor, paws waving meekly, omnivorous lips drawn back in a grin. If he could giggle, I'm sure he would. Everyone else does.

And that's just it—everyone. On many nights you know every person in the joint by name, and could tell a stranger a little (or too much) about each one. The tavern is warm because it's hospitable; it's a noisy congregation of friends, acquaintances, and neighbors. First names and nicknames fill the air; affectionate insults spice up loud greetings. You feel at home, and such familiarity is due largely to the simpler, down-scaled quality of life in the woods. Sometimes there's just more room and more time to accommodate others, particularly guests from the "outSide" world.

I'm certainly not claiming Side Lake has a monopoly on hospitality, but I think it's offered more easily here than in a lot of places I've been, and it sometimes manifests itself in ways which seem unusual, or even slightly bizarre, to city folks.

For example, we once entertained houseguests from Dallas who were blessed with the opportunity to explore the rudiments of backwoods living. We'd just moved into our new log home two weeks before, and it wasn't quite finished. There was no indoor plumbing, no windows on the second floor (only gaping holes with screen material stapled up), no electrical wiring (only a single extension cord snaking in from the meter), a plank ramp where we hoped the steps up to the door would one day be, no stove or refrigerator, plywood floors, and junk and building materials piled everywhere. The place was bare shelter, a glorified tent.

The highlight was our temporary latrine. Erring on the side of optimism, I figured we would soon install a septic system and therefore our privy need not be elaborate. I dug a shallow pit off in the brush, your basic unadorned hole, and then nailed a two-by-six to two chunks of firewood, creating a rustic bench. This straddled the pit. As a concession to the timid, I drove a steel post into the ground in front of the hole. Latrine-goers could grasp this post as they leaned back over the abyss. Toilet paper was kept in a coffee can at the site (or you could bring your own), and a shovel was there so you could discreetly cover your droppings. As a cat lover, I found this shoveling to be strangely satisfying—smart, sanitary, and wonderfully feline.

The chief drawback of the facility was the resident mosquito and horsefly population. Unaccustomed to such blatantly exposed targets of opportunity, they had a field day. I don't recall anyone lingering over the pit to peruse a magazine. Visits were businesslike and abrupt, especially at night.

Our big-city guests were used to more complicated arrangements. But paradoxically, the less means you have to be hospitable, the easier it is to provide hospitality. We had to invest a great deal more effort into their basic room and board, and it showed. Making meals without a kitchen, for example, and doing dishes without a sink, are obvious manifestations of earnestness. Daily life was more like a camping trip than the suburban residential experience to which they were acclimated.

But rural life is always like that to a certain extent. Hospitality comes easy in the backwoods; it's part of survival. Where urban folks can rely upon impersonal government, you must rely upon neighbors. And since they're relatively few, they're especially welcome. At the point where conventional necessities become luxuries, daily hospitality begins. "Tourists" are the smallest part of our guest load. It's not unusual for us to come home and find a neighbor relishing the glories of our bathtub. Our door is unlocked, and we have a water heater that won't quit. Indoor plumbing is not universal in Side Lake. (Even people with perfectly good flush toilets, some even in designer colors, will have a "biffy" sitting out back. In the summer, at least, it's a peaceful way to do what needs to be done.)

Of course it's a lot easier to be neighborly in an area where locked doors are optional. It's simpler and more practical to be open, trusting, and free with your goods if you're not worried about being ripped off or mugged. We hosted one out-of-towner who refused to leave her purse in our house unless we locked the door when we left—a sensible and mandatory practice in the city, but superfluous in the woods. I explained that if some wandering miscreant wished to enter our house while we were away, they could kick in the door or shatter the windows at leisure, not worrying about being seen or heard. Leaving the door unlocked would probably save it. She was not comforted by this reasoning: I'd convinced her that the robbers would have a lot of time to ransack the place. She thought she'd better hide her valuables, so she stashed her purse behind the couch. She subsequently forgot it there, and we had to ship it down to Iowa after she'd returned home. Her fears about security were thus confirmed: You can't trust a davenport with a purse.

While some urban visitors have been concerned about security, others have been lax with water. Even after we got a real toilet and our primitive pit, largely unmourned, was backfilled, we couldn't adhere to normal bathroom etiquette. First, we have our own well, and at the bottom is a one-half-horsepower submersible pump. Every time the commode is flushed, that pump kicks in and makes the power meter dance. At nearly 10 cents per kilowatt/hour, there's a lot of cash swirling in that bowl and headed for the drain. Second, a bad thing to do to a septic tank is to gorge it on water. The microbes that cheerfully break down sewage thrive on solids, and the less water you send to the septic system, the better (within limits, of course). So we got into the habit of only flushing when necessary. Obviously, this can be a subjective area; one person's flushing of hideous waste can be another's hideous waste. I once heard someone suggest that a sign be posted over the toilet:

> If it's brown, flush it down.
> If it's yellow, let it mellow.

We strive to be a little more discreet, but water supply and sanitation are critical, and it's permissible to be crude if necessary.

A little research shows that the concept of hospitality goes back a long way. Generally it's received a good press. Aeschylus, for instance, asked, "What is pleasanter than tie of host and guest?" The apostle Paul admonished the Romans (Chapter 12) to be "given to hospitality." But that's not always easy. Benjamin Franklin maintained that:

> After three days men grow weary
> Of a wench, a guest, and weather rainy.

Naturally I know nothing of wenches, but we can all vouch for bad weather and, sadly, for some guests as well. There is art and method to hospitality; it doesn't come naturally. Likewise, one must learn how to be a good guest. There is an implied contract in force between host and guest. In short, a host provides what he can, and a guest doesn't complain. This last is especially important in the woods. Living standards, as commonly defined on TV, are not always up to the metropolitan level. Allowances must be made.

For example, our house is dirtier than what many people (courtesy of Mr. Clean and other perverts) are used to. It's not that we don't clean, it's just a losing battle. Sidewalks, paved driveways, and lawns are not consistently available, and hence you tend to track a lot of stuff into the house. This is not unsanitary dirt, but good clean sand, twigs, pine needles, pieces of leaves, and so on, garnished with a bit of cat and dog hair.

But if you're dedicated to plush carpets immaculate down to

the roots, and tile floors that render mirrors redundant, then some of our exposed and often gritty particle board will be a bitter disappointment. One guest complained that our floors were too dirty for her child to play on. We absorbed this revelation gracefully, mentioning our fond hopes for a brighter, cleaner future. But what, I wondered, must be her opinion of the great outdoors? Surely an average playground must be far too untidy for her delicate brat. (Let them eat dirt!) This speculation was left unsaid, but that particular guest never returned. Our floors remain imperfect.

Other visitors who've holed up with us for a weekend during the winter (no one ever stays longer than that in January) have been a tad distressed at the morning indoor temperatures. Our wood stoves have their toasty moments, but when the mercury dives to 35 or 45 below zero, it's not unusual for the living room to check in at 45 degrees (above), or lower, in the morning. It's generally not life-threatening, but until I valiantly stoke the fires and the cold corners approach the 60s, some guests remain uncommunicative.

But most people have benefited from training in the art of good manners and take it all in stride. Politeness covers a multitude of sins, even when you're freezing. Besides, when we break out the blueberry pancakes, the sins can be drowned in maple syrup. (And don't ever complain about the food. Comfort levels in the corners are negotiable, but hassling the cook is unforgivable.)

In spite of, or perhaps because of, the small rigors of backwoods living, most of our guests return; and we've never met anyone yet who didn't enjoy watching our wide-screen window.

But in the winter, when the pliant summer days are a vague recollection of a half-remembered dream, you need something special—something like a pilgrimage to Hawaii, or the famous Winter Solstice Bash.

When anthropologists study various cultures, they pay a lot

of attention to the rites and celebrations—how they party. If a latter-day Margaret Mead ever writes *Coming of Age in Side Lake,* she'll no doubt meticulously record the curious rituals associated with the Winter Solstice Bash. Such arcana will be a boon to serious scholarship.

As are many plots and projects, this scheme was hatched around closing time in a local tavern. If all the plans enthusiastically made in bars were actually pursued, the world would probably self-destruct in a frenzy of feverish, and usually dubious, activity. Fortunately, most bar talk quickly fades into the ether, as ephemeral as the sound waves themselves; only a few of the more worthy undertakings ever see the light of day. Or so one hopes. Such was the case with our plans for a special party.

The winter solstice is the time of year when the sun describes its shortest arc across the sky of the northern hemisphere. It's the shortest day of the year, occurring around December 21, and is billed as the "first day of winter." Winter, of course, has usually had a substantial head start. Ancient peoples, acutely aware of celestial cycles, considered it a critical day. They realized that if the days grew too short, men would quickly perish from the earth—non-nuclear winter. Ceremonies were concocted to persuade the sun to reverse the trend and increase the length of daytime, and naturally they always worked. The Romans liked to get rowdy at the winter solstice, and their annual orgy in behalf of the cause was known as the Saturnalia. In fact, many of our traditional Christmas practices such as gift giving, the hanging of mistletoe, and the burning of a Yule log were usurped from the solstice rites of sundry pagan cultures.

So the idea of throwing a winter solstice party at Side Lake was not entirely spontaneous. Originally it was to be a *summer* solstice party (the first day of summer). A local mining engineer, disenchanted with draglines and production quotas and considering himself to be a frustrated thespian, proposed a pagan celebration which would feature himself in the role of Odin, the head honcho in the Norse pantheon. In addition to the usual culinary and fluidic excesses, we would set fire to an old wooden boat and send it floating out on the lake at dusk. It was to be the symbolic funeral pyre for all that we considered unconvivial. (If you recall, that's what happened to Kirk Douglas at the end of *The Vikings.*) We went so far as to pick out an old wooden boat, but Odin was transferred out of state and the celebration never materialized. Eventually the old boat rotted.

We were determined, however, that the Winter Solstice Bash would actually take place. Since we intended it to be a pagan festival (in a jocular way), I volunteered to be the shaman, the high priest and emcee. Having a degree in theology and an acquired taste for rigamarole, I did not consider myself unqualified. I took the role seriously. I was to address the gathering of our "tribe," setting the mood for the festivities. At last I had an opportunity to justify eight semesters of homiletics.

We slated the Bash for the Saturday closest to the solstice, about a week before Christmas. The forty or so celebrants were called upon to arrive at noon. To aid in the careful cultivation of the appropriate cultural milieu, we had a keg of beer and a hot-wine pot. Each celebrant was commanded to bring a bottle of wine of his or her own choosing, and they were all dumped into the same heated pot and garnished with cinnamon sticks (an old Sumerian recipe). Paul Masson, Carlo Rossi, the Gallo brothers, and even a farmer named Boone were all intimately mixed into a cordial narcotic. Surprisingly, it was quite tasty, but purists would no doubt have been scandalized. By prior arrangement none were present.

After an hour of meditation before the keg and the pot, facilitating the gentle correction of any straight and sober dispositions, the shaman emerged from the snowy shadows of a nearby stand of pines. I had slipped away from the libations a few minutes earlier to hone my sermon and don the ceremonial vestments. I would have preferred to strip to the waist and paint my torso with garish and offensive totems, but the temperature was around zero degrees Fahrenheit. Though I was the high priest, I had little faith in the power of the December solar disk.

So over an old gray sweatshirt symbolizing the dirty snow of the coming spring, I wore a genuine black bearskin. As is required of shamans, I'd helped to dress out the bear myself (you know, that ex-apiary hijacker who wound up on the wrong side of an unceremonious shotgun blast). As a testimonial to my ineptness with a knife, it's a sorry sight. The only confirmation that it's the hide of an *Ursus americanus* is the two teddy-like ears, which I arranged to have sticking out from the top of my head. Peering from beneath the flattened nostrils of the unfortunate bear, I had the rest of the hide draped around me in an imitation of Alley Oop. Hanging from my neck was a large, grotesque bone, the femur of a moose. I'd smuggled it out of a national park years before as a backpacking juvenile delinquent. In one hand I clutched a half-empty bottle of brandy. (Or was it half-full? We shamans have been known to ponder such questions.) This was to be my water of benediction. In the other hand was a scroll bearing the text of my homily.

I'd appointed my friend Joe to be my acolyte, my own "voice crying in the wilderness" to properly announce my arrival. He dashed out ahead yelling, "The Solstice god! The Solstice god!"

I was mortified. I was not a god but merely a messenger, a prophet. The fool! But alas, it's been a common theological error down through the ages. To minimize confusion, I didn't object to my announced status; I silently ascended my dais—a large tree stump.

Before speaking, I used a solemn finger signal to bless the tribe. It's an ancient but effective gesture, known among animists as "flipping the bird." After a suitable liturgical response from the tribe, I delivered an introductory spiel about how the sun was setting earlier and earlier, and how we must placate the sun if we ever hoped to enjoy yet another slushy, muddy, messy spring. Then with a practiced flourish I unrolled the scroll. The congregation chanted its approval when it saw the length of torn and soiled longjohns stretched between two chunks of snow-shovel handle. When the reverent uproar finally died away, I somberly read:

> *And so I summoned the elder chiefs of the tribe and I said unto them: Elder chiefs of the tribe, we must placate the sun.*
>
> *And the elder known as Paul arose, and his laughter rang through the trees like the cry of a lecherous loon.*
>
> *We must sacrifice a virgin to the sun, he said. So we searched far and wide over the land of Side Lake, but alas, there were no virgins.*
>
> *And then the elder known as Joe arose, his eyes shining like two puddles of husky urine in the sunlight.*
>
> *And he said: We must find the wisest person in Side Lake and offer them to the sun. (We wondered what Joe could possibly know of wisdom.)*
>
> *Nevertheless, we hunted far and wide, but alas, all men were fools.*
>
> *And then arose the elder known as Mike, his face red with the embarrassment of existence, and he said: We must find the purest, most righteous person in the land and offer them to the sun.*
>
> *So we searched far and wide, but alas, all men were polluted, yea, even half in the bag.*

I then rolled up the scroll (for the archives) and raising my eyes heavenward, I intoned to the congregation that the hell with it, we'd just let the sun take care of itself. I took the bottle of holy brandy, and pouring its amber contents over a nearby log, I consecrated the Yule, bestowing my blessing in the name of all "that is crude, crass, and indiscreet." The party was officially underway.

It flowed naturally into a chain-saw contest, a wood-splitting derby, volleyball in the snowdrifts, snowshoe racing, an entire roast pig, and two more kegs. Subsequent Christmas parties, usually the high points of the winter social season, were completely overshadowed. As shaman, I critically surveyed our handiwork. I saw that it was very good.

TEN

The Pitfalls of Self-Reliance

Even for a shaman, the philosophical thread connecting blueberries, chain saws, and driven wells may not be instantly apparent. However, for anyone who dreams of "living off the land," these things can help to weave a tangled web of frustration. Of course I don't know anyone who actually lives that way—independent of the modern economic infrastructure. Since the advent of *The Whole Earth Catalog* and *The Mother Earth News* in the late 1960s and early '70s, a number of folks have tried it, or thought they did. The majority of these people realized that unless they desired to crawl into a cave somewhere and exist on a level just above that of toads and salamanders, they couldn't be truly independent.

We're children of our age, fat and sassy, and we lack the temperament and motivation for true independence. And well we should: subsistence and survival, despite the high stakes, can be a monotonous row to hoe. Grubbing around in the bushes for a living does not advance the cause of civilization (using the term in all its best connotations, of course). That's not to say the so-called consumer society does either, and you can build a case that cultural decadence proceeds as an inverse square of the demand for utterly superfluous products created by TV advertising. So, many people we know are attempting to strike a balance between electric egg-scramblers and birch bark cookware. They wish to be neither completely self-sufficient nor hopelessly dependent. They're after *self-reliance*. The term covers a wide spectrum of adventure (and misadventure), but let's start with blueberries.

Human history is rich with tales of grand endeavors. Their very names have become beloved cliches, taking on the responsibility of idiom and metaphor: The Holy Grail, The Northwest Passage, Nirvana. But what blessed quest could be more sublime, more benevolent in its reward, and yet more taxing to body and spirit than the search for The Ultimate Blueberry Patch?

Oh yes, you may well scoff at these words, dismissing them as the pretentious ravings of a self-righteous hick, a misguided disciple of Euell Gibbons. If so, you have quite obviously never dipped into your cache of stored berries on a frigid January night. You haven't lovingly poured the plump, blue beauties into a bowl and inundated them with rich, white cream. You haven't lifted the spoon, trembling, to your lips and caught a fleeting whiff of summer. You haven't savored the explosion of flavor, resurrecting the hot July sun and the warm winds of August. It's moments like these that make life worth living.

Or imagine, if you prefer, a steaming blueberry pie, fresh from the oven, filling the kitchen with sensual and seductive incense. Or carry yourself to other heights, watching in mouth-watering anticipation as maple syrup flows in sinuous amber rivers across the aromatic surface of your blueberry pancakes. The mere thought creates a clamoring void within me.

There is much argument over the best way to use blueberries, and no two people seem to agree. I, for one, consider pie to be a reckless abuse of delicate berries (though I've never turned down a slice). There is but one article of faith on which all blueberry seekers are united: one never has enough. Each year I make every effort to put up twenty-five quarts. As I see it, twenty-five quarts is the bare minimum to tide us over the winter—assuming careful rationing. A hundred quarts would be better, and a jury of my peers would not consider me greedy for harboring such desire. None of us ever has enough.

And that is why we dream of The Ultimate Patch. None of us has ever seen it, yet all of us can describe it. But I'm getting ahead of myself. Before I torment myself once again by entertaining the glorious vision, I will enhance its impact by recounting the trials of the search.

It is, perhaps, unfortunate, but the primary attribute of a good blueberry seeker is an aptitude for clandestine activity. Your "good spots," either painstakingly discovered on your own or stolen from less vigilant seekers, must be jealously guarded. Friendship carries some weight, but many seekers who under normal circumstances would give you the shirt off their back become cold and distant whenever someone is gauche enough to ask them where they picked that pail of berries. In the face of curiosity, the disinformation techniques perfected by the KGB are helpful. You can bluntly send your envious inquisitors on a wild goose chase or, more subtly, say something like: "Across Highway 73 in a jack pine stand near the Dark River Hiking Trail." Those *sound* like specific directions, but in fact they only narrow down your would-be competitor's hunting ground to roughly a fifty-square-mile area. Even that's a gamble, of course, and it's probably best to skillfully change the subject by saying something like: "None of your stinking business!"

A prudent practice is to park your vehicle some distance from "your" patch and then take a circuitous route on foot, stopping periodically to ascertain that you aren't being followed. The camouflage clothing now in vogue should prove to be a real boon to blueberry seekers.

Another attribute valuable to blueberry seekers is a casual attitude toward bears. Other than predatory fellow-seekers, bears are your chief competitors for berries. The main trouble with bears is that they are indiscriminate pickers. Claws and paws are a bit clumsy, and a hungry bear (is there any other kind?) can devastate a patch in no time. Bears are even less prone to sharing than humans, and it's usually pointless to linger in a patch once a bear arrives on the scene. You must, of course, exit casually.

Heaven forbid you spill your half-filled pail.

At the other end of the wildlife scale, various noxious insects have formed a conspiracy against blueberry seekers. Mosquitoes, ticks, deerflies, and wasps apparently banded together in some remote age to prevent the harvesting of berries. Maybe they work for the bears. In any case, the customary defenses are called for—even though, as usual, they're inadequate. A capacity for suffering is a prerequisite if you wish to amass a respectable supply of fruit.

Then there are the berries themselves—a perverse lot, to be sure. Blueberries are most often small, scattered, and hidden under other vegetation. They appear to possess no predictable cycle of reproduction, and never more than a few in any patch ripen simultaneously, necessitating careful (and slow) unit-by-unit picking if you wish to avoid the additional burden of later cleaning out twigs, leaves, pine needles, and green berries. The bushes are low to the ground, and anyone with the slightest amount of back trouble is doomed to excruciating pain. And for some unknown reason, blueberries will never grow in any real abundance on your own property. Burdened by this catalog of sorrows, blueberry seekers dream of The Ultimate Patch. Details vary, but the outline is constant:

It is sometime in the future (when all good things happen). In all likelihood, I'm dead and have passed on to some more congenial place. I am blissfully wandering through a peaceful forest, yet still I feel a certain emptiness, a nagging feeling of incompleteness. Then, as I top a gentle rise and gaze out over an expanse of young pines, there it is: The Ultimate Patch. The ground beneath the trees is literally blue. The healthy bushes are so closely packed that no ferns, grasses, or thistles have been able to encroach upon them. The berries are huge, "like grapes," as we say. Six of them fill my hand. A perfect mixture of sunlight, shade, and rainfall has caused them all to ripen, and with one easy sweep a dozen mature berries fall into my pail. For more than an hour I sit comfortably in one spot, hard-pressed to exhaust the riches of twenty square feet. Every other luscious handful goes into my mouth on the spot, yet still I see that several five-gallon buckets will be required to contain the harvest. The Patch stretches out to the horizon; there is plenty for all, even the bears. A timely frost and an abundance of songbirds have dispatched the nefarious insects, and the afternoon sun is not too hot. I move lazily about The Patch, seeking out the largest, juiciest berries.

The nagging emptiness has disappeared, and I revel in "my" patch, somewhere in a glowing land where it is forever the first week in August.

It's a wonderful dream, a beautiful vision, and perhaps the Indians and the early settlers were tantalized by it as well. It would hold a special allure for someone who was gathering berries not as a mere treat but as a welcome contribution to subsistence and survival. When you're rooting around in a semi-hostile blueberry patch, you catch a glimpse of the rigors of living off the land, of the trials of true self-reliance. It's not always a pretty picture.

Still, we try. When Pam and I moved into the woods, we were determined to provide for our own needs as much as was possible and practicable. It's been a mixed effort with mixed results. I remember the time a doctor peered for a moment at an ugly gash on my left leg. He looked up and grinned. "We'll have to amputate just below the knee," he quipped.

I was only mildly amused. I could see why the man was also a deputy coroner. A certain low form of gallows humor would be indispensable.

"Fine," I replied. After all, there should be some type of chastisement for cutting yourself with a chain saw. I mean, really, how mortifying! A ragged, dirty chain saw wound is more dramatic than your average kitchen knife mishap, but so much more contemptible. I was supposed to be self-reliant, an independent back-to-the-lander with an experienced mastery of the art of chain sawing and other talents of survival. And there I was, meekly submitting to the smirking ministrations of a common MD—a man who lived in town, mowed a lawn, and probably heated his home with Arab oil.

"We get a lot of chain saw cuts," he added with an air of weary condescension that said: It should be illegal for fools to buy them, and anyone who buys one is a fool. Well, when someone is sewing up your leg for the third time in five years, you tend to agree. But only for the moment. Repentance is as fleeting as the pain.

Pam and I invested heavily in self-reliance—we cleared our own homesite, built our own house, and developed a garden plot from scratch. The purity of our experience was ruined only by the fact that we held down full-time jobs in town in order to finance this obsession. Self-reliance offers rich rewards, not the least of which is the monetary savings. You can save a lot of cash, but there are inherent dangers and inevitable (it seems) penalties.

Take chain saws. From any rational perspective they are clearly engines of madness. There are as many ways to injure or kill yourself with a power saw as there are trees in the forest. When properly tuned and lovingly sharpened, a chain saw can rip through a log or your leg with equal alacrity and disturbing indifference.

Some people treat their saws like pets. They feel that if they feed them properly (only the manufacturer-recommended bar oil), clean them (new air filter and spark plug periodically), and love them (wear a Stihl or Husqvarna cap and brag about the saw), the saws will never turn on them. Such loyalty is touching, but these people would be better served by purchasing a pair of fiberglass chaps.

Still, in the game of traditional self-reliance, heating with wood is de rigueur, and that necessitates cohabitation with a chain saw. Oh, you can buck up your eight or ten cords of birch with a hand saw, and I even tried it (briefly), but it's in the same dismal category as excavating your basement with a No. 2 shovel or listening to a speech by Walter Mondale. The sensible alternative is to buy a good power saw, maintain it properly, religiously follow all the rules of safety and common sense, and hope for good luck. You might spend the rest of your life cutting wood and never lose a drop of blood. But it's highly unlikely.

Compared to a chain saw, a wood stove seems fairly benign. We all discovered the perils of hot metal surfaces at an early age, and we aren't apt to get burned again. In addition, your average wood stove has no high-speed moving parts and few, if any, sharp edges. It's a solid, chubby, cheerful fixture, a dependable ally against the onslaught of arctic winds. In all, a good wood stove (perhaps of proven Scandinavian lineage) cuts a rather droll figure. That is, until it ignites your first—and usually not the last—chimney fire.

To the novice, this can be a nightmarish event of harrowing proportions. The once serene and steadfast stove is rumbling and vibrating, an ominous cherry-red glow suffusing the firebox like some raging intestinal disorder. It looks like something out of *The China Syndrome,* a runaway reactor headed for meltdown and a prominent place on the evening news. From your Class A masonry chimney (approved and sanctified) come sharp, distressing reports, like the sound of .22 shots. These are your fire-baked clay flue tiles popping and cracking, being summarily destroyed like so many frivolous knick-knacks in the 1600-degree blaze. Outside, the top of your chimney has been transformed into a huge and terrifying (though pretty) Roman candle, with black globs of flaming creosote spewing out and dropping onto the roof like napalm canisters. With any luck, the roof is covered with snow and you and/or the local fire department know how to handle these chaotic eruptions. You might get by with as little as $500 damage. On the other hand, the whole shebang could go up in smoke. It's advisable, therefore, to keep your chain saw out in the shed where it's safe.

Even more important than your heating system is a reliable

water supply. Unfortunately, the cost of a good commercially drilled well can be so astronomical that only Carl Sagan could comprehend the bill. Thus many self-reliant people are lured into the dubious proposition of sinking a well themselves.

The preferred method is to "drive a point." It's done as it sounds and should not be mistaken for "making a point," which is what most critics of self-reliance fail to do when it comes to wells. It all seems so seductively easy. A steel spear-like point with built-in screens is coupled to lengths of pipe and hammered into the ground until recoverable water is reached. The principle is simplicity itself, and sometimes it actually works. My own experience, however, led not to an aquifer but rather to the brink of permanent and disabling distraction.

A friend and I, laboriously wielding a 150-pound steel driver, drove a point down twenty-seven feet after only a morning's work, and there was water in the pipe. Well, that was relatively easy, I thought. But for some reason I couldn't pump that water to the surface. The consensus among various old-timers (there's always one or two around, and little in the realm of human experience, it seems, has not passed before their sagacious eyes) was that the point was plugged. This did not seem unreasonable, and so one by one I implemented the suggested measures for unplugging it.

(1) Water pressure—I pumped water down the well. Result: nil. (2) Air pressure—I forced air down the well. Result: nil. (3) Dry ice—I dropped chunks of dry ice down the well and then capped it, allowing pressure to build. Result: nil. (4) Acid treatment—I poured hydrochloric acid into the well to perchance clear the screens. Result: nil. Finally came the act of desperation. It was recommended—with a straight face—that I fire a bullet down the well. This was supposed to induce beneficial shock waves. What the hell, I did it, but by that time I was tempted to vengefully empty an entire clip into the unforgiving heart of the well. Result: nil.

Obviously there was something seriously amiss, and the only

alternative left was to pull up the point and its twenty-four feet of pipe to see just what was going (or not going) on. This was accomplished with the imaginative use of two track jacks (twenty-ton capacity), a tripod, chain hoist (three-ton), and two twenty-four-inch pipe wrenches; you know, just some of the normal odds and ends lying about in any respectable residential garage.

When the last joint of pipe was eased out of the stubborn earth, the problem became clear: the point was gone. It had broken off and disappeared, and the pipe was rammed full of sand and clay for a length of three or four feet. Small wonder we couldn't draw water through it. Apparently the point had been driven too hard, and we'd probably done it with the first dozen whacks, which had been administered well over a month ago by then.

Foolishly undeterred, I rushed out to purchase a new point. We hooked it up and dropped it into the hole, and over the course of a week we hammered it down to fifty-five feet, being careful not to hit it too hard. There was water there as well, but nothing could coax it to the surface. In lieu of further frustration, we finally called a professional well driller. In three hours he'd installed a four-inch casing down to eighty-eight feet and was pumping clear water at the rate of fifty gallons per minute. It cost plenty, but man, it was beautiful.

The entire experience was summed up for me by my friend Sooch. He once spent a good deal of time helping an elderly acquaintance put down a well. As usual, they had no end of trouble and disappointment and were seemingly devoting their lives to the project. Sooch caught the essence of it all by saying of the old man: "It's a good thing he died, or else we'd still be out there." Indeed, why prolong a life that's not worth living.

People who insist upon living the self-reliant lifestyle will probably decide, sooner or later, to build a house. For accounting purposes, their tireless labor is referred to as "sweat equity," an apt, even poetic, term. In our case it would also be appropriate to talk about "blood equity." In addition to many hundreds of normal steel nails, I also pounded three fingernails. Let me assure you, they make poor fasteners, and the pain is outstanding. They also pull out much harder than the usual 16-penny spike. In addition to numerous two-by-fours, I also sawed a thumb (though I didn't cut it off), and if I'd been awarded a dime for every sliver, scrape, callus, or scratch, we could have said of the bankers: Let them eat abstracts!

But the most thrilling accident, the greatest flouting of all that OSHA stands for, was staged by our friend Joe, a self-employed carpenter and sometime consultant on our project. He and I had just finished nailing down the second-story subfloor ahead of impending rain. We spread a plastic tarp over the new plywood, covering up the three-by-six-foot opening that would one day be a stairwell. As the hole disappeared beneath the tarp, we reminded each other to be careful where we walked.

Two minutes later, I was descending a ladder to the first floor when I saw Joe come through the tarp. While gathering up the last of the tools he had stepped into the now hidden stairwell opening. The plastic tarp held his weight just long enough for him to prepare for the drop. With a loud ripping sound, I saw his feet appear above me. Then the tarp gave way completely and Joe fell eight feet to the floor below. He landed standing up, tools in his hands. He was laughing. And yes, it is true that he later obtained a master's degree in industrial safety and was hired by OSHA. They apparently appreciated his experience.

Well, Pam and I had little of that as far as building was concerned, and while we were taking the intimidating leap into full-scale construction, we were showered with advice. The most consistent message of wisdom was *You can't do it,* with "it" referring to whatever project we were then accomplishing. For example, the whole time we were building our twenty-by-thirty-foot block basement, there were people telling us we couldn't do it. Since we were laying blocks every day, we didn't really believe them, but their skepticism caused us to proceed very cautiously. Pam painstakingly eyed the level, tipping and tapping blocks into perfect alignment. We assiduously mixed our mortar to attain the exact consistency required. We were constantly figuring and measuring and calculating. As a result, what would have taken a couple of genuine masons about two days took us a full two months.

Though we were exceedingly proud of our precision-built basement, we were still nagged by the doubts of the nay-sayers. Insecure in our achievement, we cornered a professional contractor one day and asked him, "Jim, how can we tell if we built a good basement?"

"Well," Jim replied, "when the wind blows, do the blocks rattle?"

"Of course not!"

"Then it's good enough."

And that's a key phrase to learn. All would-be self-reliant people should "internalize" that concept. Perfection is a beautiful idea, and it even has limited utility as a standard to strive for, but when it comes to construction, don't get carried away. When some future archaeologist discovers your skeletal remains, a bony hand still grasping a rusted claw hammer, you may be classified as an ancient sculptor. But don't count on it. More than likely the truth will be evident: you died from a self-inflicted hammer blow to the skull, caused by the keen frustration of trying to *exactly* center two-by-twelve floor joists. It's not worth it. Just remember: good enough! It's really quite simple, and it's just about the only part of the self-reliant lifestyle that is.

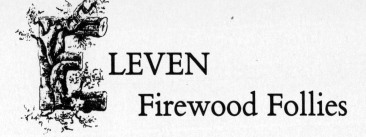

ELEVEN
Firewood Follies

A key component of self-reliance is self-defense. We have police protection in Side Lake, but it can sometimes take a while for the county sheriff to arrive at the scene. Therefore most people are prepared to defend themselves and their property, and are suitably equipped to do so. Fortunately, most local crime waves are instigated by skunks, field mice, or bears, and even if we had 911 service, it would be fruitless to call.

But on one of those rare occasions when a genuine human misdeed was going down, I found that righteous indignation and bluff are sometimes all that's required for justice to triumph.

There were four of them, all young and strapping, but I was too mad to care. Later I laughed, wondering at how crazy I'd been to challenge four men. But I didn't fear a jury of my peers. I could hear the verdict: justifiable homicide. These blackguards were stealing our firewood.

Such a low-down deed is similar to livestock rustling in the Old West—the crime transcends mere thievery. By stealing the firewood of someone who depends upon it as their sole source of heat, you are directly threatening their life. Winters are very serious business in Side Lake, where I've seen the temperature bottom out at an even −50 degrees Fahrenheit.

Besides, putting up eight or ten cords of wood is hard, time-consuming work. I've estimated that the entire fuel-gathering process, from felling trees to stacking wood by the stove, requires about fifty hours of sweaty and relatively dangerous labor.

So I was angry when we drove up our road and saw a shiny new four-by-four pickup truck parked next to our woodpile. It wasn't a local vehicle, and the four young bucks hastily tossing our winter's lifeblood into the box were strangers. Good. I'd hate to think I had neighbors who were firewood rustlers—and stupid besides. I mean, this was not top-shelf wood. These were mostly dead trees I'd cut to clear space for new growth. The stuff was worth burning only because it was handy; it wasn't worth stealing. These guys were clowns. Didn't they recognize lowbrow wood when they saw it? Now, if the pile had been good solid red oak or sugar maple, properly seasoned, it would've been worth about 21,000,000 BTUs per cord if burned in a quality stove (a cord being a volume of wood measuring four by four by eight feet). That's roughly equivalent to 235 gallons of No. 2 fuel oil. Given an oil price of $1.05 per gallon, our usual ten cords, if it was composed of such first-class hardwood, would be worth $2,585.50. We're talking grand larceny.

As it was, the dollar value of our half-punky aspen and balsam was considerably less. The rustlers were expending a lot of energy to load a measly 8,000,000 BTUs onto their truck. In deepest January, the load would keep an average local dwelling cozy for only four or five days. Naturally I've taken a great deal of ribbing on account of our woodpile.

There is a hierarchy of tree species, a sort of social register for firewood, and a fair amount of good-natured snobbery marks the woodcutting season. Our supply of over-dry or slightly spongy aspen and balsam is definitely déclassé. Though more readily obtainable in this area, both trees are at the low end of the available-energy scale, and balsam is also considered to be dirty in that it can promote creosote buildup in a chimney. Many folks who scorn our proletarian fuel are devoted to birch. It's true it has a greater BTU content, and the highly flammable paper-like bark makes for easy kindling, but its capacity for creosote formation is notorious. It's popular and widely used, but overrated—hence hopelessly bourgeois.

The real wood, the royal wood, is ash, maple, or oak. The backwoods aristocrat is fond of blathering on about the ritzy blue flames in his stove ("just like natural gas"), rhapsodizing about the heat and reputed cleanliness of these scarcer, harder-to-get varieties. As a status symbol our wood is a failure—strictly yellow flames. My defense is that it's a lot lighter (BTUs are heavy!) and affords me the satisfaction of using trees that otherwise would have gone to "waste." These particular BTUs were quite unflattering to the rustlers' gleaming three-quarter-ton four-wheel drive with chrome and pinstripe. Decomposing aspen looks scabby at best. Nevertheless, they were our scabby BTUs, dearly earned, and we were depending upon them.

When the rustlers caught sight of us rounding the bend, they leaped into the truck and fired her up. Our road is a narrow dead end, accommodating only one vehicle at a time, so they slammed the pickup into gear and plunged directly into the woods, trying to outflank us. Here was an opportunity to justify that exorbitantly expensive and commonly superfluous four-wheel drive. (Four-wheel drive is an excellent means for getting stuck in places you couldn't otherwise reach with two-wheel drive.) The wide front bumper, complete with mandatory (and unused) winch, flattened a mass of hazel brush and ripped through a stand of young aspen. All four knobby tires gouged deeply into the forest floor, casting leaves, sticks, and dirt into the air. The springtime ground was soft and the truck carved deep ruts, roaring as the driver gunned the engine and frantically spun the wheel to avoid a large stump. He wasn't quick enough. The left front tire struck it dead-on, bending the bumper and crunching the fender. The truck was literally stopped in its tracks, all four wheels whirling impotently in place, the 390 V-8 screaming in frustration. You might say they were stumped.

Ironically, some of the stolen wood in their box may have come off that very stump. It was a remnant of the previous autumn's logging, the first part of the seasonal firewood cycle. This great mandala of production is eternal and omnipresent. It's customary to keep one year ahead in order to ensure an adequate supply of cured fuel, and therefore you're almost always working at it. In the fall, I fell trees and cut them into "sticks," that is, six- to eight-foot lengths, and stockpile them until spring. Autumn is an eminently sensible time of year for logging. The weather is cool, the dirty-rotten-miserable mosquitoes and horseflies are gone, and entangling foliage is at a minimum. In addition to freer movement, you have a better chance to see wildlife. Contrary to expectations, a raucous chain saw doesn't always preclude some communing with nature. I once looked up from my noisy, smelly saw to see a medium-sized whitetail doe placidly observing me from only a few yards away. She seemed curious, undisturbed by the saw, and bolted only when she apparently got a good look at my face.

Some people prefer to log when there's a little snow on the ground, enjoying the general cushioning effect. They also maintain there's less chance of dulling a saw chain by making contact with bare, gritty soil. But this is a two-edged sword; the cushion of snow can obscure hazards. I was once bucking up a felled tree in about eight inches of snow, contentedly zipping through the trunk, confident that I had about two inches of buffer between the ground and the log. Halfway down the trunk, just as I was finishing a cut, I heard a weird ripping-grinding-clattering noise. Now what? I shut off the saw and rolled the log over. There, more than fifty feet off a dirt road which is sixteen miles from the nearest town and within the range of a timberwolf pack, was a beer can. It looked to be a yearling, just settled into a new habitat, and I'd cut it right in two. Worked wonders on my saw teeth. The quiet winter forest rang with my imprecations.

The rustlers heard something similar as I sprang out of our truck, aflame with righteous rage. I must have exuded pure menace as I stalked toward them, obviously oblivious to numbers. They could see the mayhem in my eyes. Of course they were also embarrassed, caught with their pants down, psychologically, and were therefore vulnerable. To be fair, their meekness may also have been partly inspired by our hundred-pound golden retriever. Pam had him by the collar, straining to keep him inside the cab of the truck. He was barking ferociously, his hackles high, as he attempted to claw through the closed window. Like most of his breed he was essentially a cream puff, but he could put on a hell of a show when properly motivated.

The rustlers apologized profusely, making every effort to calm this backwoods maniac and his apparently rabid dog. It was clear any tussle would result in heavy casualties. They backed the pickup out of the woods and returned to the pile, restacking their load so quickly and contritely that in a few moments my wrath had evaporated, and it was all I could do to keep from grinning and ruining my perfectly good and grim facade of hostility. I didn't expect to see those boys again.

That was eight or nine years ago, and no one's messed with our woodpile since. A couple of seasons ago I finished gleaning our forty acres of its dead trees, and I'm now reduced to harvesting high-quality fuel just like everyone else. It's a lot heavier and not nearly as satisfying, but at least we now have something worth stealing. So go ahead, make my day.

TWELVE
Chinook

It was 50 degrees below zero. But I didn't need the thermometer to tell me we were into some grim weather. It was hard to breathe outside. When I inhaled that stinging, splintery air, I coughed; and I don't smoke. The night was viscous and still, laden with skin-burning, tree-cracking arctic cold. The sky was clear and the stars were brilliant, hard and untwinkling; sharp points of icy light.

Inside, our two wood stoves roared. Despite the constant feeding of seasoned birch and aspen, the stoves were just holding their own. The temperature in the living room hovered tentatively at 65, poised to plunge the moment the fires were banked for the night. I figured that by morning the temperature in the cabin would be around 40 degrees, or lower.

Pam and I and our two guests were clustered in front of the upstairs stove, watching the flames and chuckling about the previous afternoon. Greg and Cynthia were up from the Twin Cities for the weekend, anxious to do some cross-country skiing. Unfortunately, the warmest it got, in the heat of the January afternoon, was −25 degrees. It's such afternoons that keep this area uncrowded. Skiing at 25 below isn't fun in the conventional sense of the word. The skis are stiff and squeaky, threatening to shatter at any moment, and the light and stylish ski boots will not succor your toes for very long. But there is satisfaction in it—the braving of the elements, an expiation of lazy indoor guilt.

And it makes the hot chocolate taste sweeter.

Fortunately, satisfaction can be achieved in a short time. We decided the brief two-and-a-half-mile loop of the local trail would be sufficient. It's a hilly run, and windchill was a factor. As we glided down slopes we had to keep our faces canted down or off to one side. The extra exposure of rushing air was too painful and deadly to take head-on. From deep within the hood of my Air Force–style parka I could see the trail itself and little else.

Greg and Cynthia were similarly bundled up (Pam stayed home to feed the stoves), but we still had a casualty. Just over halfway around the loop I paused at the crest of a ridge and waited for Greg and Cyn to catch up. I could see them approaching, heads wreathed with the white exhaust of their breath. Greg stopped to look back at Cyn, and then yelled and rushed to her. Cyn froze, frightened and bewildered. Greg put his mouth over her nose. I thought at first he was merely being playful, exuberant in the cold (and maybe a little weird). But I found out later that he'd seen her nose was gray—it was freezing—and he'd taken instant remedial action. Cyn was not entirely comfortable for the rest of our journey, but the subsequent hot chocolate was very sweet indeed.

We spent the evening sipping such hot liquids in front of the fire, marveling at the 115-degree difference between inside and out. It didn't seem possible. But the next morning it was 39 degrees in the cabin, and I hustled to rekindle the fires. The unofficial low, called in to a local radio station from a point ten miles *south* of us, was −57. When the rising sun hit our south windows, I heard a sharp crack, like a gunshot. One of the storm windows had split in two. Even the low, feeble rays of the January sun provided too much contrast too quickly for that particular pane of glass.

As Pam and our guests began to make muffled inquiries about the temperature from deep within their dens of quilts and comforters (the bears were certainly right to be hibernating), I turned to the gas stove with a full coffee pot. No way. The pilot lights were out; the gas was frozen in the cylinder outside. It would be almost noon before the propane would flow again. I stuck the pot on top of a wood stove and plugged in a supplementary 1500-watt electric heater to help make the kitchen habitable. The heater worked, but I'd have been only mildly surprised if the current in the power lines was also sluggish.

Greg's car certainly was. Well, actually it was dead—as immobile and dense as an icicle. When he turned the key he wasn't even rewarded with a valiant effort. Aside from a distant, ineffectual "click," there was no sound. He owned a half ton of lifeless metal and brittle plastic. He didn't even dare slam the door in frustration. I once slammed our car door at −40 degrees, and the mirror fell off. Machines are not designed to exist, much less operate, in that kind of cold.

Automobiles must be babied, so I'd had ours "plugged in." We have an electrode installed in our engine block which heats the oil to almost normal viscosity—at least to the point where it'll allow the pistons to move. Since Greg didn't have such a heater, his engine oil was more or less solid. Our car started (barely) and we tried jumping his, forcing a transfusion into his battery. We got his ignition system to make noise, but that was it. There was not enough cranking power in the universe to loosen up that oil. But metropolitan obligations beckoned, so we were determined to start his vehicle.

I filled an aluminum roasting pan with charcoal briquets, ignited them, and slipped the smoking dish under the engine block. We let it cook for about an hour, until the tray melted three inches of packed snow and ice and hit bare ground. (Real dirt, a surprising sight in January; there really is terra firma under all that snow. Sometimes you forget.) Then we jumped his car again and just managed to coax the engine into turning over. We smelled victory. We simply cranked and cranked until the motor finally started. No doubt we took years off its life. After working at it for a while, Greg even got the shift lever to move.

When it gets that cold you sometimes despair of ever smelling flowers or growing tomatoes again. Such subtropical delights seem impossible, dream-like, heavenly and ethereal. But often in January, when winter is at its bleakest, we are blessed with a warm wind, a chinook. And that fearful cold snap was no different.

The next morning it was +5 degrees at 8 A.M. Outside, the harsh, pinioned clarity of the past week was gone. The sky was gray, looking like snow, and I could see by the smoke from the chimney that the breeze was from the southwest. The arctic cold front which had swept down from Manitoba was being displaced by warmer air all the way up from the Gulf of Mexico. By noon the temperature had risen to 16 degrees, the warmest we'd been for over two weeks. At sunset it was 21, and the mercury didn't fall after dark. Now there was a good sign—the southern winds could overcome even the long winter night. We turned in at midnight, and the temperature was up to 27 and rising.

At dawn it was 34 degrees, and water was dripping from the eaves. Icicles as cold as the North Pole only thirty-six hours before were now decomposing as if it were fresh and noisy April. I ran outside, where it smelled like spring, like aspen buds on the verge of life, or puffy clouds on the verge of rain. There would probably be a garden again, sometime. But I wasn't fooled. The wind had quartered to the west, no doubt on its way to the northwest. The day would grow a little balmier, but I wouldn't bet on another warm night.

I climbed onto the roof to clean the chimney, taking advantage of the momentarily cool wood stoves. It was the only time in January when they wouldn't be too hot. It's uncomfortable and hazardous to be brushing out a flue when it's still spewing hot and noxious gases.

When that chore was done, I slapped on my skis and floated through the woods. It was 40 degrees, and the trail had softened just enough to make it slick. With no hat, gloves, or long underwear, I felt as if I were snubbing obligations. I was like a kid playing hooky. And man, what a glide! The slightest pressure on my skis and poles and I was flying—sliding and zooming through the forest—over ridges, down valleys, leaning into curves, and shooting halfway up steep hills. Occasionally sunlight would break through the overcast and slant in among the pines, lighting up the snow and feeling positively tepid. Five miles of trail flashed beneath my skis in less than an hour, and I barely broke a sweat. It was fast and smooth and almost silent. I was past before the squirrels knew I was there, and the air was so warm, so breathable; it didn't hurt to fill my lungs.

But toward the end of that soaring ride the clouds began to move out en masse. The breeze was cruising in from the northwest, and a new cold front would bring another frigid and crystalline night. In an hour the sun was free, shining bravely in a clear sky. There was a little heat, but soon the sun was on the horizon, orange and weak. By the end of twilight the temperature was in the 20s. At midnight it was zero; in the morning it was −15.

But there had been a promise in the southerly wind, in the warm westerly air. And a chinook doesn't lie: there will be flowers and tomatoes again. Yes. Though spring seems incredibly distant. I read the weather section of the newspaper and notice that places like Hawaii and southern California enjoy the same balmy temperatures day after day. I imagine that those subtropical citizens ignore their local weather reports. Such benign and stable conditions would be nice to experience (in moderation), but boring to hear about.

It's the opposite in Side Lake. Everyone pays attention to the weatherman, especially in the winter. People take a morbid interest and a masochistic pride in how ridiculously cold it's going to be for fifteen or twenty solid days in a row; or how many inches of snow driven at how many miles per hour will choke the roads by dawn; or how close to −100 the windchill factor is going to be.

Over morning coffee down at the store, citizens exchange

thermometer readings, vying for the twisted honor of having the lowest temperature. It's amazing how much they vary. One person's backyard may have bottomed out at −41 degrees, while the nearest neighbor, barely a half mile away, only dipped to −33. The latter must therefore endure good-natured scorn about living in "the banana belt." "Take that thermometer off your stovepipe," someone will quip, and the store will echo with gentle chuckling. It's not a bad place to be on a cold winter morning.

Up here a store is a place where you drink coffee, exchange gossip, complain about the climate, and cordially hassle the proprietor. You don't really "shop," since you pretty much know what they stock and how much they want for it. You do buy things: staples such as dog food, Miracle Whip, and shotgun shells. But the reckless impulse to buy isn't as common as it is in a seductive metropolitan department store. (Though I once picked up an extra splitting maul handle on a whim—I couldn't resist the attractive wood grain—and my old one wasn't even broken.)

Local merchants don't get carried away. These are not the gilded repositories for the latest gadgets featured on TV. Karl Malden notwithstanding, you may safely leave home without your American Express card. And a "mall" is something you use to split firewood. But even here, at 48 degrees north latitude, a mere 18 degrees south of the Arctic Circle, you can now rent VCRs and videocassettes.

It's had an impact on winter. Let's face it, if you're at home on a long, dark, cold winter night, your options for entertainment are limited. When the reading, conversation, and sex peter out— some enduring longer than others—you're left with *watching:* the fire in the wood stove, the plummeting mercury, or as a last resort, the television. Trouble is, most households around here can pull in only one or two channels, and the standard network fare is usually a shortcut to a terminal case of ennui.

But suddenly, it's showtime. You can now run down to the

store and pick up anything from James Dean to Molly Ringwald, and view it, as they say, in the comfort of your own home. Assuming, of course, that your home is comfortable. (Did you put up enough firewood this year?) Some folks would rather be down at the tavern. Though we haven't conducted a scientific survey, Pam and I are willing to bet that VCRs have put a dent in the local tavern trade, at least in the winter. It's easy for inertia to gain a foothold when it's below zero outside and showtime inside—with movies for every taste. Though I must tell you that X-rated videos are currently unavailable in Side Lake. Pornography must be imported from town.

But winters are persistent enough to enervate our appetite for movies, and when electron overdose becomes acute, we fall back on our charter membership in the Side Lake Demon Society (SLDS). No, we aren't in the clutches of some satanic cult, enmeshed in weird rituals and sacrificing small animals. "Demon" is a particularly wild card game, and what we're sacrificing is the integrity of our nervous systems.

The rules are simple. Four or more members (we've had as many as eight, but attrition is high), each with his or her own deck of cards, gather round a table and psyche themselves up into the proper mood. The ideal mental state is an alert, high-pressure tenseness closely resembling the attitude you possess when your compact car hits an icy spot on the highway and you skid into the oncoming lane of traffic, just missing a loaded logging truck.

Each combatant takes thirteen cards and stacks them in a pile, face up. This is the "demon pile." Then four more cards, also face up, are laid out singly next to the demon pile. By convention, as the last member finishes arranging his cards, the game is launched. The object is to be the first one to get rid of your demon pile. You do this by feverishly examining every third card in your deck, using them to play solitaire on your four single cards, and casting all aces into the center of the table. You may then play on any of these aces as well as on your own cards, always alert for a chance to rip a card off your demon pile and place it somewhere else. With five players, there can be as many as forty ways to play any given card, and the arrangement before you is mutating rapidly and continuously, five hands streaking from decks to the table in a frenetic flurry.

In sixty seconds you've got the pulse rate of a hummingbird. Hands collide in the center and cards fly off like shrapnel. Three or four players race to slap a deuce on top of the same ace, all arriving at once and crumpling cards into pathetic wads. Hands dart, dodge, and slam, peeling through decks as fast as possible and tearing away at demon piles, while eyes jump and scan and heads bob and weave.

Rastus starts to hyperventilate as the tension builds, not sitting in his chair but perched on bent knees, hunched over the table like a hunting raptor. Speedy, as apt as his nickname, whips through his frayed cards in a stiffened state of taut concentration, pounding them home with authority. Nancy, who infected us with this obsession, plays quickly but lightly, flicking and fluttering her cards like chickadee wings; but she is not without talons. Pam slaps and groans, entangled in a love-hate relationship with the brutal game. We're all talking at once, cursing and insulting the competition and loudly bemoaning our own misfortunes, miscues, and lost opportunities. It's a lot like real life: not good for the blood pressure.

But the reward of victory is sweet. As the last card vanishes from your demon pile, you triumphantly shout *"Demon!"* and then relish the groans and imprecations of your victims. Metastasis. Deal 'em up! We're talking winter here, and anything that keeps the blood vigorously pumping is not to be sneezed at. In the summer we play bridge.

And it will come. The brief warm wind of January is a cousin to the hot, sultry breezes of July. But hey, there's nothing really *wrong* with winter; it just stays too long—a once-appreciated guest that wears out its welcome.

And that happens every March. Around here winter usually begins the first or second week in November, and except for a few fanatics, we've all had enough by the end of February. But it is not to be. March is a sadistic tease. Just when the temperatures are beginning to mellow out and some of the snow is melting, we'll be hammered by a blizzard that violently deposits eighteen inches of fresh stuff and is immediately followed by a 20-below cold snap. Weather Bureau records show that March, the month that boasts the first day of spring (ha!), also has the highest average snowfall—it beats January by a mile (or at least by several inches). It's the final test of sanity and soul.

But almost every year one wonderful thing transpires in March. First, after a few days of sunny afternoons in the 40s and 50s, the snowbanks are wet and mushy from top to bottom (usually a span of about twenty-four inches). Then one night, when a tongue of cold air creeps down from Canada, the temperature drops to zero or below and the snow refreezes, "welded" into a hard, solid mass. That means you can ski right on top, without breaking trail, anywhere. Wherever there is snow, in forest, meadow, or swamp, you are completely free to travel, gliding easily where you would have painfully wallowed at any other time during the winter. You have the power of total access and it's a heady opportunity.

When the snow becomes crusted like that, I set off to explore the wild country to the west of our cabin. There's a lot of muskeg and swamp back there that is inaccessible most of the year. On skis I "skate" over lakes, ponds, and other open areas, pushing and poling from side to side, building up speed and flying over the sparkling crust. As I penetrate the wooded swamps, thick with black spruce, I ease up and gently slide between the trees, poking ahead with my poles.

There are deer tracks everywhere, and I'm pleased to see the snow is hard enough to support their weight as they search for browse. Soft, deep snow in March can be extremely tough on the deer herd. When they're coming out of wintertime semi-hibernation and starting to feed more heavily, struggling through deep snow can sap their strength and lead to starvation. I also notice the local porcupine population is active: I see a half dozen jack pines and Norway pines have been stripped of their bark from stump to top. From a distance they stand out on higher ground like strange albino trees, pure white trunks in the midst of shadowy woods.

I emerge from the swamp and dash down an old logging road, an abandoned right-of-way being slowly retaken by the forest. Several red squirrels flee across my path as I skate along, racing and jumping to the safety of spruce boughs, and then angrily chattering at this human apparition, this invader who is violating territory which has been sacrosanct since last fall's hunting season. They're in the middle of their first of two yearly mating seasons, and I hope I haven't interrupted anything important.

Just before I angle off the road and back into the muskeg, a snowshoe hare leaps away from behind some alder brush and fires for the woods. I notice its white winter coat has splotches of gray and brown, a sure sign of spring. After I stop to watch the rabbit disappear, I see a small hole in the snow a few yards ahead, and I mosey over to investigate. The depression, about eight inches deep and the same in diameter, contains a pile of tubular, brownish-yellow grouse droppings. They look fresh. I don't see any of the distinctive three-toed tracks, but the crust is probably too hard for a grouse to leave any. I circle back around, heading into the muskeg, and right at the edge I flush the grouse out from under a balsam tree. There is bare ground at the base of the trunk, and the bird has been crouched in the sunshine, feeding on nearby buds. With wings beating and tail splayed, it flies off into the trees and brush behind me. It looks fat and energetic—as if it wintered well. Perhaps we'll meet again next autumn.

I glide over a wide expanse of swamp, encounter a narrow, frozen stream, and follow it to a small woodland lake of ten or twelve acres. At the mouth of the stream, where there had probably been open water only the day before, the snow is packed with fox tracks. It looks as if at least two of them had been by for a drink, or one that had danced around for a while.

Kicking for momentum, I speed across the flat snow-covered ice, skating hard and grinning. This is a lot of fun, and I know it's also winter's last hurrah. The next time I'm on this lake there'll be a warm wind tugging at the prow of my canoe. I can live with that.

THIRTEEN
Other Waters

The rivers open up first, their treacherous ice dissolving into the freshening currents. While lakes are still locked up with dark and dying floes, you can slip your canoe into the river and paddle toward summer. The first canoe ride of the year is a rebirth, a flowing and gliding passage out of the deep womb of winter. The water is very cold, a degree away from ice, but it is water. It's free to absorb sunlight; it's free to make waves.

We say a river has a source, that it springs out of something else. In a word, it is born—continuously. Every moment, a river is replenished, distributing water downstream. It passes life along and the living congregate on its banks, sometimes dramatically so.

It was just after sunrise, but you could barely tell it. The early morning mist was lying thick on the river and visibility was about thirty feet. Pam and I were slowly paddling our canoe upstream, hemmed in to a narrow channel by alder brush and cattails. The current was slow and the water placid, clear, and cold. We were careful to keep our paddling noiseless. Only the red-winged blackbirds disturbed the stillness of the dawn. Besides the soft hiss of our hull slipping through the water, birdsong was the only other melody.

We moved gently upriver, happy with the morning. Then abruptly there was a loud crashing off to our left. So sudden was the noise that we started, shaking the canoe. Something big was smashing through the woods, and the ruckus was growing louder by the second. We stopped in the water and waited, our eyes intently focused on the brush at the bank. In a moment the branches burst apart and a large whitetail buck leapt out over the river, his antlers held high. From an altitude of five or six feet he plunged into the water about two canoe lengths ahead. For an instant he was under, the water surging up to his rack, and then his head and back broke the surface; there was wildness in his eyes. He was just starting to swim across when he saw us. Apparently what was behind him was less frightening, for he immediately turned and pushed back to the bank from which he had flown. Noisily splashing, he struggled into the woods and was off. The peace of the dawn was shattered and gone, but we weren't disappointed. It had been a pleasant surprise.

That's the nice thing about rivers—you can never be sure what's around the next bend. And even if you could, the knowledge would soon be obsolete. Rivers are dynamic, metaphors of change. Heraclitus, the prophet of flux, wrote, "You could not step twice into the same river; for other waters are ever flowing onto you." It's these "other waters," of course, the current and flowage, that keep things interesting. They erode banks, deposit sediment, carry debris, and rush over rocks and down hills to form rapids and waterfalls. The volume of these waters can make fishing good or bad, a valley lush or parched, a stretch of white water pretty and benign, or pretty and deadly. We like to see a river rolling along, going somewhere, doing something, evoking a sense of purpose.

Once we paddled a 116-mile stretch of a local river, almost its full length. Before leaving, we had to find a place to cache our vehicle for the duration of the journey. There was an old farmhouse near the bridge where we planned to enter the river, so we approached the elderly man who lived there and asked him if we could store our truck in his yard for a few days. We explained our intended trek, and his eyes took on a wistful glitter as he gazed at our canoes. "I've always wanted to do that," he said, yearning in his voice. But the itching was gone. "Well, c'mon," replied one of my buddies. But we could see it was too late for the old man. He would continue to watch the river as it flowed past his house, watch it as he had for decades, wondering what was downstream. Maybe it would add a year or two to his life.

When you spend time near a river you want to get to know it better. Where does it go and how does it get there? What lives in it and on its banks? How fast is it? But most of all, what does it *feel* like?

This is especially true of violent water. A frothing, tumbling rapids is magnetic. People stare at cascades and cataracts, fascinated. What would it be like to be in that water, a flung and flowing part of the torrent? It's a strange, scary urge, akin to the odd temptation we often experience on cliffs, bridges, or high buildings—what would it be like to jump off? Our lust for experience sometimes carries us to the edge of life.

In the case of a flying, suicidal leap, the best you can do is approximate it. A high dive or a parachute free-fall can give you an idea of the sensation, but it cannot be exactly the same as a spontaneous jump from a great height—which you can usually experience only once and for all. (But take heart. As my parachuting instructor once said, "It's only the last half inch that hurts.")

Similarly, to know a river, you can get on it with your canoe and become part of the current, part of the purpose. You can even paddle into a stretch of white water and shoot the rapids. But it's not exactly the same thing, either; unless, of course, your canoe capsizes. It can be a pleasant surprise.

John and I were paddling down the Vermilion River, intending to "do" some white water. We arrived at a spot known as Liftover Falls, a name indicating to many people that it would be the better part of wisdom to portage the canoe, experiencing the river from the safe (and irrelevant) shore. Though safety was not our objective, we did stop at the portage to stash our lunch in a dry place and survey the layout of the rapids.

The width of the stream was constricted to about thirty feet, less than half of normal, with the whole volume of the river trying to fight through. There was a four- or five-foot vertical drop within a twenty-foot length of wild water. It was more of a short, steep slide than a falls, and it dumped into a turbulent stretch of flatter white water which immediately made a bend, surging against large boulders. All told, from the top of the slide to the relatively still water around the bend, we had thirty yards of rapids and very strong current. The water was deep and the bottom rocky.

It was apparent there was an easy route and a difficult route over the slide. To the right, it was less steep with a lower volume of water, and looked like a good practice run before we shot the more intimidating left side. In the center, the flow was split by a huge submerged boulder, ominously black.

We paddled several yards back upstream into stable water, and then pivoted to face Liftover Falls. All we could see was the foaming lip of the rapids and the flat river beyond. From even a short distance it appeared as a hairy perpendicular drop. We approached slowly, ruddering nervously with our paddles to ensure a proper, straight-on entry. John was in the bow, and as we glided past the point of no return, he let out a loud and comforting whoop.

We picked up speed and flashed over the rim of the slide. For an instant the prow of the canoe was out of the water, hanging over the edge, and then we plunged down the falls. At the base of the slide the powerful, raging stream curled back on itself, raising a mad white wave as the water tried to go in two directions at once. Our canoe dived into this wall of water, and for a moment it was touch and go. Would we continue downward, "submarining," and be totally swamped? The water broke over the bow into John's lap and washed back down to my ankles, filling the canoe about a quarter full. Then the prow kicked up and we hit the crest of the wave, "surfing" out of the slide. We both whooped.

We paddled furiously through the choppy current, battling to clear the rocks and make the bend. We used our paddles to deflect the canoe from one slab of granite and missed another by inches, but we reached calmer water intact. Hurrying back to the portage, we emptied the canoe and studied the left side one more time. We figured we had the feel of the water. There was no doubt it was a more dangerous run, but I was confident we would make it. Granted, we might ship a little more water, but other than that . . .

We concluded later that our keel hit the lip of the slide at a bad angle, and we never properly corrected. We were dead meat from the start. The canoe shot down into the wall of water cocked to one side, and we hit hard. The prow did not pop up, but burrowed into the standing wave. For one ridiculous moment the disaster seemed to unfold in slow motion. The canoe gradually tipped past the point of equilibrium and then *wham*, we were gone. I, John, and the canoe were all shoved into the foam and sucked underwater. Now this is what the river really felt like.

It was about eight feet deep at the base of the slide, and my right knee and a hand bounced off the rocky bottom. I was tumbled in a somersault, like a leaf in a high wind. My eyeglasses were strapped to my head, but the force of the current ripped them halfway off. Even underwater, I grabbed for the frames and shoved them back on, the reflexive result of years of conditioning. There was a beautiful, weightless sensation of moving very swiftly through the bubbling water, and then I was spit to the surface.

John, the canoe, and I all bobbed up at the same time, about twenty feet downriver. John's cap was gone and he was laughing. The canoe was full of water and hanging just below the surface. The current gripped us, dragging us rapidly toward the rocks in the bend, and it was all we could do, kicking with our soggy shoes, to push the loggy canoe into a small eddying backwater out of the main flow.

John and I crawled up onto slimy rocks, looking half drowned. My knee was bleeding. But we both still clutched our paddles and we laughed joyfully, beat-up but euphoric. Abraham Maslow would have called it a "peak experience." We knew what it was like to be part of the torrent. It was a pleasant surprise; that's the nice thing about rivers.

But that was in temperate and charitable July, a beneficent month, when the water is warm and the rivers are low and forgiving. The favorite time of experienced white-water paddlers is late April and early May, when the rivers are brimming with snowmelt and early rain, surging against their limits.

Emboldened by our summer exploits, I was impatient by the end of the following March, anxious for the ice to break up and be gone. I wanted to hit the rivers at high water, riding the crest of spring. But if I could have foreseen what kind of excitement was in store, I might not have been so gung ho.

In the last week in April, John and I chose the Sturgeon River as our first challenge of the new canoeing season. Its source is Side Lake itself, where it begins as a flat and meandering wild rice bed, sluggishly curving through marsh and bog. The stream is placid for several miles, an easygoing home for mallards and muskrats.

But when the course narrows and the banks rise, the Sturgeon is punctuated with long stretches of boulder-strewn rapids. It's a clean northern river, the wild runs framed by mature, towering spruce. From the wooded banks you can see the Sturgeon slanting toward (ultimately) Hudson Bay, rushing downward over rocky slides.

When we drove up to the bridge where we'd decided to put in, my stomach fluttered and my mouth dried up. One hundred inches of snow had finished melting only two weeks before, and heavy rains had followed. The river was swollen and turbid, hurrying under the bridge with foam-flecked menace, tugging at trees along the bank. It appeared to be at least three or four feet higher than when we'd last been on it, the previous September. This was a faster, deeper, more powerful stream, and the water, so recently freed of ice, was only a few degrees above freezing.

We'd been joined in this venture by Neil, a veteran runner of rivers, and as we donned life jackets I could see the bright anticipation in his face. It was clear he felt this river was going to be wild enough to afford him pleasure, and that was another ominous portent. He would be alone in his canoe, so to aid in tracking through the water, he placed two rocks in the bow next to his cooler of beer.

It was a couple of miles downstream to the rapids, so I had about twenty minutes to contemplate the mission. I was less excited than I had been, a little cowed by the force of the current. Yes, we'd run this stretch before, but in low water. How would the character of the run be changed? There should be less maneuvering involved, since most, if not all, the rocks we'd dodged last fall would be well submerged. On the other hand, what fancy moves we did perform would have to be executed more quickly and surely since the current was much faster. John said the only thing worrying him was a short but steep drop he remembered toward the end of the rapids. No doubt it would be extremely treacherous in this volume of water and we must be alert for a way to avoid it. Right on, bro. I recalled the spot and tried to imagine how it would look now. I pictured a pile of water resembling Liftover Falls, and it scared me. The river was now literally cold enough to kill.

The soft snugness of my brand-new life vest made me feel a little braver. I'd never owned one before. In twenty-plus years of lake canoeing, I'd never felt the need—canoes don't sink and they're eminently stable, even in whitecaps. But this arctic-cold river was another matter. We could laugh while swimming at the base of Liftover Falls, pursuing our capsized canoe through sunny July water, but the Sturgeon in April was a harsh and burly place devoid of summer mercies.

We saw the first standing waves from about a hundred yards off, and I motioned Neil over to the side of our canoe. I tunneled into his cooler and found a can of pop amid the Stroh's. My mouth was still dry, and the cool sweetness felt good. To cover my nervousness I joked about a "last drink," and we all grinned like fools, denying the comment any claim to accuracy. I placed the empty can on the deck behind my seat, and Neil pulled away, eager to be in the rapids. John and I peered ahead, choosing a path.

We could see no rocks. The river was a mass of white waves from bank to bank, the current tumbling over itself in a rush to get through. None were very large, and we rode over and between them with little trouble. But every time we cut through a two-foot whitecap, tossed a bit from side to side, we were sprayed with cold water, shipping some into the canoe. After a quarter mile of this swelling, gushing fight, enough water had slopped into the canoe to make handling a little difficult. It sloshed around as we rolled through the waves, pulling at our stability. I dug deeper into the river, paddling hard to compensate.

I yelled to John, noting that if we took on much more water it might get rough. This was something of which he was no doubt aware, but in a minute it was irrelevant. Neither of us saw the steep drop until it was too late. We'd been seduced by the main current, lulled by its apparent evenness, and we followed it to destruction.

Our critical mistake, of course, was in not hiking along the bank and scouting the run. But it was a long walk, and we'd run the stretch before, and we knew the drop was there—somewhere. However, a spring river and an autumn river are distant cousins, only remotely related. We should have treated that run as a complete unknown. We didn't, and we paid.

We were about one canoe length from the drop when I knew we were done. It was a mad and churning cataract, a standing explosion of foam and spray. Our prow plunged in and down, and the canoe was instantly flooded by one huge wave. John was looking *up* at the crest, and just before I was yanked under, I saw the water surge down past his neck and swallow him.

The shock of the cold was paralyzing. I popped to the surface immediately, but I couldn't breathe. I felt as if my chest was clenched inside a giant, malevolent fist. The current was incredibly strong, gripping my legs and trying to pull me back under. For several seconds I gasped and choked in vain, unable to get air as I was dragged downstream. I thought that in spite of my life vest I was going to die, frozen and drowned. I started to panic, almost sick with fear, and then I managed to draw a breath.

It calmed me a little, and I noticed the stiffness in my arms and legs. I could barely move them as I tried to dog-paddle to keep my head up. John was ten yards to my right, closer to the middle of the river, and clinging to the swamped canoe. He had a very serious expression on his face—a pinched and wide-eyed combination of fear, pain, and determination. I supposed my face looked the same. He yelled to me, but I couldn't make it out over the roar of the river. Just then my feet and legs started bouncing off boulders and I tried to establish a footing, struggling to rise and barge for the bank, only twenty or so feet away. But the current was overpowering, sweeping me along before I could stand, keeping the shore out of reach.

Neil whipped by in his canoe, an arm's length from my bobbing head. He'd found a path around the drop; violent, but runnable. From within the grasp of the frigid, pummeling river, he looked like a free and flying bird.

"You all right?" he asked as he passed.

I tried to say I was okay, that is, alive; but I was too cold to speak. My throat was hard and knotted and no words would come. I started to reach out and grab the gunwale of his canoe, the instinctive gesture of a drowning man. But I stopped short, realizing it would be neither polite nor smart. There was no sense in endangering Neil (the competent bastard!) or, as he would no doubt mention, his cargo of beer.

But you can't loiter around in water that cold for very long and expect to live. What finally saved us was a bend in the river. The current directed us toward the inside bank and we fought the rest of the way. After two or three minutes of uncontrolled flowing and thrashing, we finally felt a submerged clay bar beneath our feet and half swam, half crawled to the edge of the woods.

John pushed the canoe to within my reach, and I helped him drag it into calmer water near a deadfall that extended into the river. We turned it over to empty the water and then shoved it up the bank into the brush. We clambered out of the river and stood in a sunny spot amid the trees. John complained that his hands were numb. I complained that my aluminum canoe didn't look the same. I hadn't noticed until we hauled it out of the water, but it was bent to the starboard side, skewed for its entire length; and the hull was pocked with several new dents. I remembered a tidbit I'd read in a white-water guidebook put out, appropriately enough, by the Red Cross. A swamped seventeen-foot canoe in a current moving at 5 mph (which Neil guessed this was) can be assaulted by hydraulic forces exceeding 2300 pounds. Small wonder you see them folded in half along riverbanks. I should feel lucky, I told myself; my canoe was no longer pretty, but it was still serviceable.

Neil pulled his canoe onto the bank and tossed up the paddle I'd lost at the drop. He'd managed to scoop it up as it rushed by him in the waves. John had hung on to his, but my extra one, a lovely new paddle which I didn't use in the rapids because I didn't want to bang it up, was gone—washed out of the canoe.

Neil came ashore and we hiked downriver through the woods, doing what we should have done before, reconnoitering the way ahead. My first impulse was to portage the canoe back upriver to calm water and return the way we'd come. I'd been deeply impressed by the authority and vigor of the rapids. But upstream paddling sounded too much like work to my comrades, and they insisted we should run the rest of the white water. There was only about a hundred yards of waves left, and then it was a lazy cruise to the next bridge and the truck we'd left there. Besides, Neil said, we might catch up with my new paddle somewhere on its wayward journey downstream. That appealed to me.

As we eased the canoe back into the river I was on the point of shivering. The breeze cut viciously through our soaking clothes, and the thought of another spill into the current was terrifying. Be cool, I thought, and then snickered to myself. John and I were about as "cool" as you can get. We safely, though nervously, negotiated the rest of the rapids, a stirring anticlimax, and a little later overtook the can I'd emptied just before we entered the waves. Hopes rose that we might find my paddle as well, but it wasn't to be. Someone will find it, a glossy new paddle floating downstream or hung up on a snag. And if they understand rivers at all, they'll know its story. It's not surprising.

FOURTEEN
The Incomplete Angler

There is more to rivers than adventure, excitement, and fun. There's also fishing.

I don't fish as much as most of my neighbors do. You see, I had an unfortunate experience as a youngster: one day I caught nine fat walleyes in a matter of minutes. Recovery has been slow.

The main thing about fishing is that there are as many theories and axioms about technique and style as there are people who fish. Many are contradictory. Listening to fishermen is like listening to philosophers—just more confusing. It would be nice if they were more like physicists, working at developing a Unified Theory of Angling. That, however, is unlikely. Over three hundred years ago Izaak Walton wrote *The Compleat Angler,* and obviously it wasn't complete. For example, there was no mention of electronic depth finders, and the advantages of a graphite-epoxy rod were ignored.

The closest I ever heard anyone come to summing up all fishing knowledge was when one of my angling friends, who had just been skunked on a usually productive lake, finished his third beer and said: "That's the funny thing about fish—they're just like people. Sometimes they bite and sometimes they don't."

That made sense. I don't know about you, but I seldom bite. If fish are like me, then that explains my lack of success. Except for that one time, of course.

A couple of my uncles had taken me and some cousins up to

Lac La Croix on the Canadian border. It was back in '65 and perhaps there were more fish around then. In any case, on the first day we hit a hole. In less than three hours on a magical, unbelievable afternoon, our party of five landed over sixty eating-size fish, including a seventeen-pound northern pike that was forty-three inches long. That sucker looked as big and predatory as a barracuda, and there was some doubt expressed about the wisdom of heaving it into the boat. When it flashed by under us, distorted by refraction, it seemed as if it required several seconds for all of it to pass. My uncle from Illinois finally subdued the monster, and it was, I think, one of the highlights of his life. He and the pike made the papers back home.

We camped on an island, ate all the fresh walleye we could handle, and then triumphantly brought home five limits of fillets. It was fantastic, and it spoiled me rotten. I returned to the real world believing that was the way fishing was supposed to be. Subsequently, if I ventured out and didn't get a bite in a half hour or less, I gave up in disgust. Over the years I've been working my way back into the sport, but rehabilitation has been painful.

Getting married didn't help. It turns out my father-in-law is one of the world's great fishermen. A dedicated veteran who firmly believes you need to put in a lot of time on the water, he always carries two rods. That way he has a spare in case one pole is shattered by The Big One, and he can have a different lure on each rod and switch tactics quickly. He also carts around a tackle box that qualifies as luggage. And he's got the touch. He and I once sat in the same boat, with the same bait, fishing at the same depth; he caught ten and I caught diddley-squat. I began to wonder if there was a psychic component to successful fishing. There definitely is a hereditary factor. Pam is a fanatical angler, equating time on the water (or ice) with true living. Most other time is a series of fuzzy parenthetical spans between fishing excursions.

As proof of her zeal she has recently sought entry into the

relatively small, tightly knit fraternity of fly-fishermen. These people are the freemasons of fishing. They operate in esoteric realms beyond the ken of the average weekend angler. Using bits of dead animals (fur, feathers, hair), hunched over small vices "tying flies," they construct their own lures. They indulge in sacrifice. It's not unusual for fly-fishermen to slice open the first catch of the day and examine its stomach contents—reading the entrails, as it were. Once they see what the trout or bass have on the menu, they can delve into their little box of amulets and find a handmade lure to match.

You can't fish out on the fringe like that without becoming an elitest. This was made plain to me when I accompanied Pam on a long pilgrimage to the best fly-fishing store in Minneapolis. It was a Saturday morning in early March and the store-temple was full of people who knew each other by name. It was too early to be out on (or in) the water (since it was all still frozen over), so instead they were talking about it and spending substantial amounts of money on gear. Amassing necessary (and unnecessary) quantities of gear accounts for fully 50 percent of the fishing experience, even for the elite.

Behind the counter was a pleasant young woman who greeted folks as they entered—chatting, kidding, and making them feel at home. She obviously knew a lot about fly-fishing and appeared to be happy and cheerful that she did. Then the phone rang. She answered it, bright and friendly, but in a moment I saw her whole expression change. Her smile vanished, her brows drew together, and her voice turned to ice. "No!" she spat into the receiver. "No, we don't!" And she hung up. "Can you believe that?" she announced to the faithful. "Some turkey wanted to know if we sell *live bait!*"

There was a chorus of snickers and snorts. If God wanted humans to fish with live bait, He would have given them all worms. (Or shiners.) Later I went into the bathroom and discovered that over the toilet someone had hung a fairly nice watercolor. It showed a handsome trout on the verge of biting into a hook with a juicy night crawler attached. The painting was titled *The Ultimate Heresy*.

I cringe to imagine what the artist would think of my friend Sooch. One year he decided to get his seasonal fishing experience "out of the way early." After buying a license, he went to a gas station in town and asked the attendant for one minnow.

"You mean one *dozen* minnows?" the man asked.

"No," Sooch replied. "I mean *one* minnow."

The man was so nonplussed he gave him his one minnow for free, oxygen pack and all. Sooch then marched over to a hardware store and purchased a rod, reel, line, bobber, sinker, and one hook, for a total of $12.95. He then ventured out into the bush, nestled into a good spot on a bridge over a local stream, affixed his single shiner to his single hook, and on the fourth cast "the reel flew farther out than the bobber." Disgusted, but also curiously satisfied, he tossed the rod into the river after the rest of the tackle. Good. That was done for another year, and he was proud of his technique.

Of course all anglers, regardless of how they fish, figure they know what they're doing. If their particular stratagems don't work, they can always blame it on a host of variables, from water temperature and wind velocity to the color of the boat. That's why fishing is so satisfying. If you're successful, you're successful, and there's no ambiguity. If you're not, you can justifiably blame it on something else; and besides, you may choose to define success in your own way. A good day may consist of merely getting out on the water and not hearing a discouraging word—from anyone. If a five-pound largemouth bass decides to join you, well, so much the better. You must assume the bass knows what it's doing as well.

But anglers should not assume too much. In *The Compleat Angler* Walton wrote, "Angling may be said to be so much like mathematics that it can never be fully learnt." For anyone who's struggled through differential calculus, that's a humbling thought indeed. Personally, I've always considered fishing to be a bit far-out and non-Euclidean. How else to explain the continued geometric growth of "the one that got away"?

But I'm being unfair. Fishing is beyond sport and diversion. It's a means of transcendence, a way of easing the burdens of life en route to an enlightened state. It's beyond the vulgar criticisms of neglected spouses and others of the unconverted. The devoted angler longs to cry with Shakespeare through the voice of Mercutio: "O flesh, flesh, how art thou fishified!"

FIFTEEN
The Dark Side
of Nature

I can see it in the headlights, fluttering and doing little loops in the air. It's a long way off but we're closing in on each other rapidly as I cruise down the highway. What a welcome sight as it dances through the halogen beams and then shoots over the hood of the car. Splat! Spring is smeared on the windshield. It's the first squashed bug of the year. Many people wait longingly for the first robin melodies or for the first glimpse of an out-of-state license plate, but one of the surest signs of approaching warmth and sunlight is an insect-splattered windshield.

The other sure sign involves B-26 water bombers. Between the time when the snow vanishes and the time when the grass, ferns, and bushes turn a moist, fire-resistant green, we live in a tinderbox. The DNR (Department of Natural Resources) calls it "fire season," and if we have a dry spring there are going to be brush fires and forest fires on a daily basis. Smoke in the air means spring.

A few years ago, on a warm afternoon in early May, I was out in the garden preparing the soil for the summer campaign. I was engrossed in a rock hunt, ferreting out the fresh crop of stones which seems to appear each spring, pushed up, they say, by frost. I ignored the sound of the aircraft at first, assuming it was just a small spotter plane patrolling the woods for plumes of smoke. But soon the distant drone grew louder, resolving into the distinctive sound of twin engines. I began to look around, and the buzz became a roar. The B-26 came diving out of the east, thundering by directly overhead.

Gee, it's flying pretty low, I thought, as it swept over the lake. The plane was less than two hundred feet up, and when it reached the forest just beyond the lake, a great wave of water surged from its belly and cascaded toward the treetops. I gasped. The B-26 was on a bombing run—less than a mile from the house! The haze I'd noticed earlier was really smoke.

As I climbed to the roof of the cabin with a pair of binoculars, Pam called the local DNR station and they told her they'd been trying to contact us with a warning about the blaze. We weren't directly threatened yet, but it was possible.

Perched on the peak of the roof and leaning against the chimney to steady myself, I focused the binoculars on the woods to the west. I could see the smoke clearly now, but no flames. As I watched, another B-26 swooped into the haze and dropped a load. It spread out on the breeze as it fell, slashing toward the ground in an iridescent band—like distant, sun-streaked rain. It looked imposing, but I couldn't tell how much effect it had on the fire, or even how extensive the blaze might be. But the wind was not in our direction so I felt secure for the moment.

Pam and I discussed what we'd toss into the pickup if we were forced to evacuate. First on our list were our personal files and records—titles, deed, birth certificates, manuscripts, et cetera. The diary I've kept for twenty years was high on my list. Pam thought of her handmade quilts, a few favorite books, some clothes, the stereo. Then there was the canoe, the typewriter, skis and hockey equipment, the chain saw, tools, fishing gear. And what about the sofa, the only piece of furniture we'd ever bought new? And the stamp collection, don't forget that. And what about . . .

It was soon clear that the less time we were allowed to mull it over, the better. Given more than three minutes, all the junk you own becomes essential. We'd have to evacuate via Mayflower.

By dusk the DNR figured they had the fire under control, but several hundred acres were smoldering and the leading edge of the blaze was not completely extinguished. When it got dark I returned to the roof, looking for an orange glow, but all was darkness.

That night I had a terrible dream. A wall of fire, driven by wind which showered sparks ahead of the flames, came ripping and crackling through the woods. From our upstairs window we could see it reach the lake, pause, and then start to spread around either shore. Spruce trees lit up like torches, blazing in a swirling stream of smoke and sparks. The flames raced along the ground as fast as a man could trot, devouring dead grass and ferns and flying up the pitch-laden trunks of the balsams. The fire crowned out, leaping from the treetops and arcing into the sky. Three deer bounded through the garden in panic, fleeing the smoke and the red-orange demon.

It was obvious we had only a few minutes to get out. Already sparks and flaming bits of debris were landing on the roof. We could feel the air growing warmer. We stumbled downstairs, bolted for the pickup, and as we sped down the road our evacuation cargo consisted of the dog, the cat, and a filing cabinet. Less than a mile east of our house we ascended a high hill (which does not exist). Nightmares are well equipped for torment, and this figment of my dream provided us with a perfect view of our cabin. It was burning. Flames were leaping up every wall, curling around the eaves, and shooting across the roof to merge in a wild and snapping inferno. The dry logs were ideal fuel, burning with fierce intensity.

Those walls we loved, that coddled us on windy winter nights and soothed us on rainy days, were blackened and half devoured. The numberless hours of toil and sweat that had arranged the logs into our home were now nullified. I felt my body sag under the realization that we'd have to start over. Then the dog barked, and I woke up, frightened and depressed. It was 3 A.M. I got out of bed and peered out the window to the west. There was no trace of flames, and the fire was no doubt still under control, if not beaten. Still, in the morning I phoned my boss and got the day off. I needed to hang around the homestead just in case; the vivid dream had convinced me of that.

But even that wretched scenario was not as bad as Pam's recurring nightmare. Ever since we moved into our cabin she's regularly suffered through this shocking dream: The noise of heavy equipment awakens us, and when we rush outside to investigate, we discover to our horror that someone has established condos or a trailer park right next door. A bulldozer is mangling aspens, tearing them out of the earth to create a highway and a parking area. We fly into a tortured rage that wakes Pam up for real.

Fortunately, residential development isn't a likely prospect. It seems that just about everyone who can live around here already does. That's enough. When the temperature drops to −40 at Christmas, or when the mosquitoes descend in a rapacious cloud in May, I feel a twinge of gratitude. If there were few bugs and if the winters were not so bitter, there'd be 5 million people living on the lakes between Duluth and the Canadian border. And it wouldn't be worth a damn.

When you've achieved our level of friendly isolation, sheltered from noise, traffic, and general human clutter, you guard it jealously. We're vigilant, wary of proposals for hazardous-waste sites and nuclear repositories, but nature does most of the work. Four months of hard polar-like winter, and two or three more months of what is considered winter by most of the rest of the nation, serve as an effective buffer.

I like to think of nature as an ally, but in fact she's neutral. And that neutrality is not benign. The fairness of a forest fire means destruction to all in its path. There is a dark side to nature. If you flip through the pages of a colorful book from the Sierra

Club, you won't see it. If you take a weekend hike in a park, it probably will not be revealed. But if you live in the woods for a while or spend more than just a few days on the trail, nature will often drop her mask. She's beautiful, but basic to the fiber of the forest are death, terror, and misery as well.

Take rabbits. What could be more benign than a cute little bunny frolicking in the woods? But what is a rabbit? Season after season, it's food—and the harvest is never gentle.

On a warm and moist July night we're rudely awakened by piercing shrieks. From out of the mist around the lake come scream after scream, in a regular, horrible tempo. In the daze of sudden wakefulness, my first image is of some terrified woman being brutally murdered. But the screams are too regular, too inhuman. They go on for a solid three minutes, then abruptly cease. Another wounded rabbit has painfully and noisily died. It takes a while for sleep to return.

From a low rise blanketed with late November snowdrifts I can watch the drama unfold this time. The grayish-white rabbit runs full-out for several yards, halts briefly under a snag, then makes a long, graceful jump to the left and stops dead in the snow. Its nose and ears are twitching; its eyes are wide open and blank. Behind, the dog is barging through the snow, his nose glued to the track. He never even looks up as he closes in on his quarry. The rabbit remains motionless in the snow, and the dog bumps into it nose first. He grabs it in his jaws, and with a single violent snap of the neck the rabbit is dead. The dog finally looks up. He wags his tail.

There are a set of rabbit tracks in the December snow. They lead from the edge of the aspen woods out across a meadow. But near the middle of the clearing they stop. The paw prints just end, and no rabbit is in sight. What's this? It's puzzling until one sees the faint marks next to the prints: two sweeping, broom-like swaths in the snow. Wings. With talons like dagger points, an owl has snatched another rabbit from the face of the earth.

Standing by the back door I see the cat emerge from the tall midsummer grass at the edge of the yard. She is drenched with blood. Alarmed, I run to her, but find she is unhurt; it's not her own blood. Over the next few days, a half dozen dead baby rabbits appear next to the kittens on the back porch. Later, only the tiny furry feet remain.

After all this, the rabbit seems an essentially tragic figure. We've all heard the cliches about the fertility and rapid multiplication of rabbits. It must be this way, because so many of them are appointed to die at frequent and regular intervals. Like the plankton in the sea, they breed and reproduce to serve as fodder for everyone else, or so it appears. They are the cute and furry grazing grass of the forest, born to die young. If the north woods can be likened to an engine, then rabbits are a source of fuel.

But nature hides more than blood and scattered entrails behind her radiant facade of inspiring sunsets or quiet, limpid pools. Her latent hostility can be expressed in more subtle and unnerving ways: the wind, for example. It's not for nothing that in many ghost stories a haunted house and a howling wind are inseparable. On a windy night it's not the noise of the wind that disturbs us, but rather the noises it may obscure. Our ears probe the gusts as an animal uses its nose. We're like hidden deer searching for whispers of danger. What noise is that upwind, merging with the rustling of trees? What is downwind, aware of us? What frigid, killing front is moving in from the Arctic? What great pressures, as vast as continents, are causing harmless air to take on force and a roaring? On windy nights it's best to be indoors, by the fire.

But nature thrives on sound, and her dark side listens to more than screams and death rattles. Why, for example, is the wolf so hated? Is it that the haunting strains of the wolf cry touch a chord of fear in the human mind? To hear a melancholy wolf howl drifting over the trees on a moonlit October night is to hear the echoes of a primitive dread which has never been reconciled. It reaches our very blood as the heart skips a beat. In tense and silent anticipation we await the next eerily melodious notes. Are they closer? What wellsprings of the animal soul produce these sweetly tortured songs of the wilderness? For these spine-tingling howls are not the battle cries of the predator but the fatalistic pangs of a noble prey. They speak of lonely, frozen lakes, and the lean, hungry nights before death. They reverberate along the forlorn trails of solitary individuals beneath the moon, mingling notes of joy and sorrow in a single tune of finite life. They define a tenuous captivity aching for a ephemeral freedom. What fear is heard when the wolf sings? What somnolent ghost is awakened in the recesses of the mind? Perhaps it's the spectre of our own vulnerability, our own suppressed anguish with a lonely imprisonment, our own longing for a freedom which neither we nor the wolf can realize. The wolf boldly sings a song which many have feared. He taunts us with the lyrics of our dirge. For this he must die. Killing is the charge, but howling is the crime.

But in the end, of course, the wolf is at home. He has his niche, and being an intimate part of the ecosystem, nature holds no surprises for him. She shouldn't for us, either, but over the years our concept of the woods and the wild has been sanitized, homogenized, and endlessly rendered to pap. Full-color postcards, brilliant and beaming, announce "Wish you were here!" But you aren't always welcome.

During an especially severe winter a few years back, I headed into the woods one day, intending to hike out a way and spend the night. It was late March and mild, but there were still about three feet of snow on the ground. When I left the house, it was clear and sunny. The snow had a thick, hard crust, and walking was easy. I ambled along a familiar trail, taking my time and noting the first faint traces of spring.

An hour before sunset I was still a good distance from my intended campsite, and clouds were moving in fast. The wind took on a keen, cutting edge, and I was out of the crusted area and into soft drifts. I had not brought snowshoes along, and I was wallowing in waist-deep snow and struggling uphill. My pack was beginning to weigh heavily on my shoulders. It would be dark soon, and colder.

Then the snow began to blow in. I was suddenly in a closed little world, walled in by gusts and flurries of snow. Except for the moaning wind and my own labored breathing, it was utterly quiet and increasingly dark. The shining and lighthearted mood of the daytime was gone. The unexpected weather had made things difficult, brooding, and a little dangerous.

I stepped into a hollow beneath the snow and fell forward. I lay there a moment, resting, and as I began to rise I noticed a speck in the snow, close to my face. I peered through the deepening gloom and realized with surprise that it was a dead fly. I hadn't seen a fly for four months; they simply aren't around in the winter. Apparently the mild temperatures had brought it out. The first hint of spring had lured it from some unknown hideout only to kill it in the colder hours of dusk. A great, overpowering loneliness overcame me, and for the first time in my life I felt remorse for a dead insect. In the warm summer days I'd slaughtered annoying flies with a vengeance, but there in the snow I mourned.

For a few moments I felt a strange, sad kinship with the fly. Its fate was a common one: lured out in the bright warmth of day, it had died by betrayal at sundown.

A sharp gust of wind stung my face. I scooped out a hole in the drift and buried the fly. I headed up the hill and left it behind. Nature would kill me just as easily and just as indifferently, if she got the chance. There is no remorse in the northwest wind. Nature is beautiful and sometimes benevolent, but she plays no favorites.

After living in the forest for several years, I understand the inclination toward nature worship. I'm not a professing pagan, but I can see that "our" trees are more than mere yard ornaments. They're sources of life—the very material, in original form, that constitutes our dwelling. They provide the fuel that keeps us from freezing, and which occasionally cooks our food. They are shelter and sustenance for the wildlife we sometimes eat. They deflect the brunt of stormy winds and trap the blowing snow that would drift in and bury our road. Wild plums, pin cherries, and crab apples can be plucked from their branches.

On the other hand, trees can also be elements of disaster. They can be blown over, falling across roads and roofs. They can attract a bolt of lightning, and by means of trunk and roots, lead the strike to us. (As members of the fire department we once saw how this happens to a house. A charge conducted by roots shattered windows, blew paneling off the ceiling, and ignited a fire inside a wall.) They can be engulfed in flame and transmit the killing fire for miles.

All these things, the good and the bad, are inherent in the character of trees. There is some source for trees which is beyond our ken and control. Yes, we may plant trees, and Pam and I have added fifteen hundred seedlings to our forty acres, but we cannot create a seed. Here is a great gap in our knowledge and ability. Even in this age of bioengineering there is mystery in the reproduction of life. And even if the biological process is one day minutely decoded, if DNA is unraveled to the nth degree, there will still be the most intriguing question: How did the process begin?

When Druids worshipped in oak groves, the quest of their poetry had the same end. And in the verse was the understanding that men and trees, men and nature, are part of the same stuff. There is coexistence, dependence, and the kinship of the living. When I see a deer springing through dense forest on a misty autumn morning, unobstructed and floating, as if leaping through the hearts of trees, I feel a deep longing. I wish I could do that—run and dodge like a buck, flying at full speed through tangled, unnoticed corridors which twist between the aspen and spruce.

Or to be like an eagle—would I watch my wingtips as I soared in spiral orbits high over blue water? I imagine seeing my feathers splayed, feeling the lift of air, the power of invisible currents in the transparent sky. My body is light, weightless between long, broad wings. My head is free to roam, scanning the distant water, probing beneath the sparkling surface. My eyes have lenses that make the world sharp, focusing on the flashing glint of each ephemeral sparkle, resolving them to tiny points of light, and then slipping behind to the refracted shadow of a wiggling fish. I create a sudden gust of rushing, cooling wind as I bank and aim my beak toward the earth. The sun lays a sheen on my back as I hide in the path of its rays, tucking in for a silent, deadly dive. There is a great force at the bottom, a heavy tugging by the mass of the planet, fighting the steep curve of my plunging descent. And then I extend my wings again, feeling the pressure of flight on the feathers of my pure white tail. For a few swift moments I skim the surface of the lake, then quickly dip, and stab talons into the water. There's a cold splash and then an instant of mushy resistance before my claws meet in the middle of a redhorse's belly. A brief thrashing, a flash of fins in alien air, and I lift the throbbing weight out into the atmosphere, wheeling for the tall pines.

And thus the ancient Celtic bards sang beneath the oaks:

> I am a stag: of seven tines,
> I am a flood: across a plain,
> I am a wind: on a deep lake,
> I am a tear: the sun lets fall,
> I am a hawk: above the cliff,
> I am a thorn: beneath the nail,
> I am a wonder: among flowers,
> I am a wizard: who but I
> Sets the cool head aflame with smoke?

That was the goal of the wizard, of the shaman, and of the priest: to be all things. What better way to understand them? To "be" the wind, stirring up deep waters, requires a leap of imagination, an expansion of mind which cannot fail to attain a level of transcendence. Through the ritual of observation—looking, touching, listening—we come to know the world. One is not enlightened by doing obeisance, by paying dues, but rather by paying attention. The apostle Paul wrote: "For whatever is to be known of God is plain. . . . God himself has made it plain—for ever since the world was created, his invisible nature, his everlasting power and divine being have been quite perceptible in what he has made." The liturgy is simple: stop, look, and listen. (That is the secret of wizards.) Earth and sky are brimming with revelations, and sometimes all you must do is step outside and look around—especially at night.

One evening I saw a very bright meteor. It appeared in the north, a brilliant red fireball bursting into the atmosphere and streaking down from the zenith toward the southwest. It left a smokey, rust-colored trail, and after burning across a third of the sky, it exploded.

There was no sound, but the meteor fragmented into three pieces, each flying off in a different direction and leaving its own brief trail before abruptly winking out. The main trail remained visible for a moment, lingering in the dark against the stars before gradually fading away. The whole spectacle lasted about three seconds—a very long time for a meteor—and when it blew up, a bystander would have heard me gasp, "Wow!" It's a pious word, filled with praise and thanksgiving.

For there is a reservoir of wonder in a dark, unobscured night sky. Without haze, without lights, the backwoods sky is a translucent black. It sparkles. It draws me outdoors before bed; it attracts my eyes and holds them, and when I lie in bed I gaze out the windows.

I saw the meteor because I was looking. Darkness is a blessing—it helps you to see. It's a backdrop for the spectacular, for sights that seem like visions. Coupled with quiet and solitude, the night sky can be overwhelming. It's little wonder that's where humans have seen their gods and demons.

For example, one of the most astonishing things in the northern sky, the aurora borealis, or northern lights, was called *jee' byug neemeid' dewaud*—"dancing ghosts"—by the Ojibway. And ghostly they are. Though glimmering oracles from the solar furnace, harbingers of the nuclear fires at the center of the sun, they make no sound. Though they are spawned by the solar wind and outline the magnetic field of the planet, they are utterly silent. One would think such powerful manifestations of celestial potency would roar, howl, and grind with natural authority. But the aurora is noiseless. In dazzling radiance, the leaping flames are mute. Surely this is something ominous. You await the inevitable explosion that never comes. You watch the ghosts of the Ojibway ravage the sky without a single word or cry. In hushed splendor the northern lights upset the night, coming and going in amplified silence.

This spellbinding sight of luminous shimmering infects the mind with a sense of mystery. Bright rays, vibrating in expansive walls of light, inspire wonder. Lofty pines, backlighted by pulsating, shining arcs, draw you to the northern horizon and the secret polar regions beyond. Sometimes the entire sky writhes in rays and arcs of a rich and blazing emerald green. Sometimes you see an undulating curtain of vivid red, fantastic and unreal. From horizon to horizon the heavens are a tapestry of light in a dynamic state of flux. The color and movement blend into an awesome choreography of sublime chaos. It's raw beauty. It's the spirit of the north, conjured out of darkness and dancing wildly to the music of cold silence.

Mark Twain, a man who paid attention to the sky, wrote that "Grief can take care of itself, but to get the full value of a joy you must have somebody to divide it with." And so my friend Sooch and I have an agreement that whenever one of us sees the northern lights, no matter what the hour, he is to contact the other and spread the good news. You hate to miss a fine display. Part of their value is that you don't see them every day (around here, about twice per month on average), and the longer it's been since the last aurora, the more anxious you are to see one.

That's one reason I certainly didn't want to miss that other renowned celestial show—Halley's Comet. Unless I live to be 111, it's a one-shot deal. I explored a vast quantity of the available literature and it all emphasized the necessity of dark skies for comet hunting. I felt smug about that. We wouldn't have to mount a minor expedition to escape the enshrouding glow of city lights.

So I obtained a plot of Halley's course from an astronomy magazine, and on November 13, 1985, I spotted the comet for the first time through binoculars. It was a dim, hazy patch of light near the clustered Pleiades, still too far from the sun to sport a tail. It was an unspectacular sight in itself, but exciting nevertheless. It was like seeing a movie star in person—a titillating view of an otherwise unremarkable human who has been celebrated and hyped. I remembered reading about Halley's Comet as a child, noting the awe and hysteria generated by the last visit in 1910, and performing a quick calculation to see how old I'd be in far-off 1985-86. Thirty-five years old—it had a decrepit and hoary ring to it, but I guessed I'd make it.

When I glimpsed it for the first time, tiny and modestly faint, I understood Halley's true value. It's a calendar. Like so many celestial objects, we use it to mark time. In an instant my life telescoped back to about 1964. I re-entered the mind of a thirteen-year-old kid who was fascinated by the stars. I could see the page in the *Sky Observer's Guide,* my first astronomy book, where there was a photo of Halley's Comet and a table outlining its past and future appearances. I vividly recalled the wonder and enthusiasm, the unquenchable curiosity and optimism. It was more than a memory—for a moment I was *there,* and the intervening twenty-two years were as nothing. I felt a tingle ripple along the back of my neck. It was the sensation of time travel; the occasional, slightly giddy feeling we experience when we actually realize we are individual mortal beings with a real past and a certain future. It's the phenomenon that produces a tear when we think of lost friends and deceased dogs.

But Halley's flashed me back without sorrow. I found I could look at a dim dot in my binoculars and still get excited about it. I could see precisely how long twenty-two years was, but I hadn't aged all that much—yet.

A few evenings later some friends came by to play cards, and when there was a break in the action, we trooped outside into the cold November night and let our eyes adjust to the enveloping darkness. Then I pulled out the 7 × 50 binoculars (suitable for U.S. Navy night watches) and one by one we saw the comet. Except for Rastus. He couldn't see through the binocular eyepieces with his glasses on, could see even less with them off, and never did get a fix on Halley's. It was maddening for him to listen to us discussing that little blob of light, that smidgen of history and physics, and not be able to see it. He focused and refocused the lenses until his fingers were freezing and his neck was stiff from craning upward. In a way, he experienced Halley's more intimately than we did. He explored the comet's territory in his imagination, and he'll remember it for as long as the rest of us.

After studying Halley's we did some time traveling of a different magnitude. I pointed out the Andromeda Galaxy, one of the closest cosmic neighbors of our own island universe, the Milky Way. In a dark rural sky it's a naked-eye object, a hazy beacon among hard, glittering stars. Through binoculars you can distinctly see the oval shape of a spiral galaxy.

Speedy was captivated, amazed to realize that Andromeda is supposed to be 1.5 million light-years away and contain 100 billion suns. The combined light of those stars, the image we were seeing from out there in the yard, took 1.5 million years to reach our retinas. Theoretically, the galaxy could no longer exist and we'd never know. Just by looking up we were swept 15,000 centuries back in time. Speedy felt the tingle. He wanted to memorize the galaxy's location so he would be able to show it to his young nephew. I pointed out the four stars in the Great Square of Pegasus, one of the most prominent asterisms in the northern sky, and how he could use them to find the pattern of stars in the constellation of Andromeda, and hence the galaxy. The constellations are bright and their paths are easy to find in a dark sky. He traced the configurations with a finger, his arm raised and outstretched toward the heavens. He was a discoverer with a new map. I envied him. He'd just seen the universe grow; his vision had taken a quantum leap. His mind had been dosed with the equivalent of a shot of adrenaline—it was excited, expanded, sharp. That doesn't happen every day.

But it often happens at night. Under a clear dark sky.

SIXTEEN
Surprises

Life in the north woods falls into a seasonal pattern. There's a time for woodcutting, a time for wood burning; a time for planting tomatoes, a time to hide them from the frost; a time to hunt for deer, a time to hunt for ticks; a time to plug in your vehicle, a time to unplug your sinuses. The climatic extremes enforce a certain regularity of yearly events that allows for little deviation. For instance, if you put out those tomato plants in mid-May, you may certainly kiss them goodbye. Old misanthropic Jack Frost has booked several more gigs before mid-June.

Added to nature's cycles is the rhythm imposed by ourselves: town board meeting the first Tuesday of the month, fire department meeting the last Wednesday, cribbage at Riverside Inn every Tuesday from January to March, mail arrives at the post office at around 11:00 A.M. Life might become routine, perhaps even dangerously rutted, if it were not for the regular occurrence of irregular events.

There was the late August evening when we received a breathless phone call from an acquaintance who lived about seven miles to the southeast.

"A plane just crashed into the lake in front of our cabin!"

Pam was still a reporter at the time, and I was doing freelance photography for her paper, so we rushed out to the car and raced over dirt roads to Dewey Lake. We pulled up to the shore right behind an ambulance and a deputy sheriff's car. It was drizzling and misty, with a very low ceiling, and the lake was gray and foreboding. It was a poor day for flying.

The woman who'd called us pointed to the area where she'd last seen the single-engine Cessna, upside down in the water. It had sunk quickly and no one had surfaced. The county rescue squad was not yet on the scene, so I borrowed a small boat and rowed out to the crash site. Dusk was approaching and the water was turbid after heavy rains, but I could make out the tail section of the plane just below the surface. It looked as if the cockpit must be twelve or fifteen feet down. The plane had been underwater for about a half hour, and it was conceivable someone might still be alive, trapped in an air pocket—if they hadn't been killed on impact. I entertained some fleeting, foolish thoughts about trying to dive down and drag people out, but even if I could hold my breath that long, I'd be able to see little or nothing without a face mask and an underwater light.

Three motorboats pulled up and grimly circled the wreck. "We've got to *do* something," someone said, and a heavy-set, authoritative-looking man eased his boat over the submerged plane and slipped a towline around the tail section. The other two boats followed suit, and they revved their outboards in concert, trying to tug the wreck into shallow water. It wouldn't budge.

"The nose must be stuck in the mud," another man said.

There was yelling from shore. Three local scuba divers who happened to be on Dewey Lake were preparing their gear for a dive. In a few minutes the rescue squad boat arrived and hauled them out to the plane. It would be dark in an hour, and the divers hurried over the side and kicked for the bottom. After a short time one of them surfaced, yanked out his mouthpiece and gasped, "There's two bodies down there—we're bringing them up." He disappeared again.

Another boat cruised in, cut engine, and joined our somber and silent flotilla. No one seemed to be breathing as the six boats gently bobbed in the cold drizzle. Everyone stared at the water and waited. The tail section was a ghostly blob beneath us, growing less distinct as a wet and chilly night descended. Ten minutes passed—time enough for the tenseness of our morbid vigil to grow painful. I imagined the horror of being in the plane as it came down, knowing you were going to hit the cold, gray water; knowing you would probably die in that rainy, gloomy lake.

A diver suddenly broke the surface alongside the rescue squad boat. He grabbed a rung of the boarding ladder and then pulled hard with his other arm. A limp and sodden mass emerged from the water. A second diver appeared next to it, and hands reached down from the boat. The divers extended the bare, pale arms of the corpse, and the men in the boat grasped them and heaved. A spectator hissed, "Damn!"

The victim's mashed face rubbed against the hull of the boat, leaving a trail of blood. The rescue squad got the body halfway in and eased the torso to the deck before pulling on the legs. For a moment they stuck straight out from the gunwale in a macabre and ridiculous attitude, as if part of some tasteless slapstick. Water dripped from the toes of the white tennis shoes.

I viewed it through the lens of my Pentax, struggling for a clear focus in the misty dimness. I concentrated on exposure and depth of field and wondered how the other spectators were filtering the horrible image. I was a predator and that soggy body was carrion—I recoiled by focusing in. This was not a man, a human like me; it was merely a subject, part of the composition of a news photo. It almost worked. I delayed the shock for a few seconds, squeezing off frames and temporarily blocking a lucid and inescapable vision of mortality.

The second victim was brought up immediately, and his ashen face was curiously unscarred. It was terrifying. He looked intact, very human; possibly asleep. But he was dead—gone off into deep darkness. My lens was no help at all.

I didn't sleep well that night, but in the morning the photos were there, secure inside my camera. They proved to be hot items. They were wanted by UPI, two law firms, an insurance company, and the FBI. We learned to our surprise that the two victims were FBI agents, and they'd been on duty at the time of the accident. Other agents showed up at Dewey Lake asking about a briefcase. When it didn't turn up on the salvaged plane, they hired the three local divers to search for it on the bottom of the lake. They couldn't find it, and the FBI brought in Navy frogmen. They combed the area for a couple of days, and when they finally located the briefcase, said our friend on Dewey Lake, the FBI agent in charge was "very happy." All we ever found out was that it was a matter "involving national security," and that was an off-the-cuff comment by a federal agent. As far as I know, no official statement as to what the FBI and their briefcase were doing in our quiet and sparsely populated area was ever released.

Naturally there was a lot of speculation, some of it fired by the fact that Walter Mondale, then vice-president of the United States, occasionally spent time at a friend's cabin on Dewey Lake. Was there a connection? We'll probably never know. Anyway, it was an extraordinary event, a bolt from the blue—like the night we volunteers received a fire call from outer space.

It was early February, and cold, about 25 degrees below zero. It was the kind of night during which you say, "I bet we get a fire call." Fire fighters grow cynical after a short while, expecting alarms at the worst times. They are rarely disappointed.

The alarm came through at about 7 P.M. I was at the hockey rink when one of our members pulled up and told me we'd been paged with a strange call. The dispatcher had said that a passing aircraft, of all things, had reported "a large blaze" ten miles southeast of Bear River. That put it smack in our laps, and several volunteers scrambled for the fire hall. But "ten miles southeast of Bear River" didn't exactly nail down a set of coordinates, and for a moment confusion reigned. Had anyone seen a fire on the way to the hall? Had anyone been called with more specific information? No. The fire could be anywhere in our jurisdiction.

Well, there was no sense in lumbering around the region in our fire trucks while the water froze in the tanks, so we fanned out through the woods in our own vehicles, looking for what must be one hell of a fire to be called such from the air.

And what a frustrating, helpless feeling. Every minute counted, and we didn't even know where the fire was. Besides, if it was someplace very far off the main roads, we could drive by and never see it. What if lives were in danger? The situation had the potential to make us out as buffoons, perhaps tragically so.

And then the dispatcher called again, and the new word was passed along. The blaze hadn't been spotted from an aircraft, but rather from a NORAD satellite! Now *that* was a fire. But, he added, a small mistake had been made. The disaster was not ten miles southeast of Bear River, but ten miles *north*east. That placed it over fifteen miles beyond the limits of our coverage. We heaved a collective sigh of relief. The conflagration was someone else's problem.

But it finally came down to no one's problem. The sheriff's department searched the indicated area that night and all the next day, by land and by air, and discovered nothing. No one anywhere knew of any fire, and no smoldering ruins were found. Well, said NORAD, it must have been a large meteor; and that was eventually the official conclusion. I guess they don't call large meteors fireballs for nothing. And it was comforting to realize that the North American Aerospace Defense Command is indeed looking out for us. They should understand, however, that if they get a fix on a Soviet bomber over Bear River (ten miles one way or the other), the Town of French Volunteer Fire Department doesn't want to hear about it—especially if it's 25 below zero. Meteors we can handle, but NORAD will have to deal with the Russians themselves.

One might expect to be surprised by NORAD or the FBI. They are, after all, alien entities as far as Side Lake is concerned.

But when you're viciously attacked by a grouse—a small, timid, and harmless woodland fowl—the world seems dumbfounding indeed.

It happened on a backwoods trail in late June. I was about six miles into a twenty-five-mile hike, and my main travails had been rain and mosquitoes. Intermittent showers kept me soaked and kept the trail greasy. And as I slipped along over wet rocks and squished through clinging mud, I was doggedly pursued by a voracious army of mosquitoes. As long as I was moving briskly it was bearable. Three or four per minute would dive into my face and I could slap them without breaking stride. The noxious high-quality repellent I'd smeared on my skin may or may not have helped. After an hour it was hard to tell. The layer of chemicals was covered, and apparently superceded, by a slimy coating of crushed bugs.

Killing the vermin (with extreme prejudice) brought little satisfaction. I knew that no matter how many I destroyed, my efforts were insignificant. This follows from Eino's First Law: In June in Minnesota, at any given point at any given time, there is an infinite number of mosquitoes. (Eino's Second Law is $E = mc^2$: "E," Eino's misery, equals "m," the number of mosquitoes in billions, times "c^2," cursing squared.)

I could sense this truth on the trail. As I strode along I'd glance over my shoulder and see the mass of mosquitoes right behind me. I was being hunted and run down like a rabbit. I was actually their prey—they lusted for my blood—and it was not an entirely cheerful sensation.

But not nearly so cheerless as when I finally worked up the courage to stop for a breather after five miles or so. In an instant I was blanketed by attackers. I felt the horde of insects press against my skin. They were flitting around in my eyes, in my nose, and when I tried to steal a swig from the canteen, in my mouth. I waved, flailed, swatted, and danced in a frantic circle until I managed to get a little water (and three mosquitoes) down my throat. Then I was off at full speed, hoping for higher ground and a stiff breeze to keep the bloodsuckers at bay long enough for a snack. (Mine, not theirs.)

In self-defense, I was rapidly sinking into an altered state of consciousness, mechanically hiking along, eyes pasted to the trail as I rhythmically slapped mosquitoes and vividly imagined that lofty granite palisade where the amiable wind would sweep my enemies away and bright sun would dry my clothes. A couple of short miles later, when I saw the grouse in the middle of the trail just ahead, I ignored it. It was merely another object in the path, like a rock or a root. As I approached, it calmly (or so it seemed) walked off to my right and disappeared into a patch of dripping ferns.

But when I drew abreast of the ferns I was violently ambushed. There was a furious flapping, like a swift tattoo on a snare drum. It rose up from my ankles and darted for my head. I jumped aside, startled and uncomprehending. My first thought was of mosquitoes—a giant (some mutant wilderness strain engendered by nuclear testing) had me dead-to-rights and I'd have to strangle the sucker, locked in hand-to-proboscis combat. But then the grouse was right in my face, a feathery berserker with pounding wings. I felt the sharp gusts of air as it plunged in toward my neck, savagely attempting to peck at me. I assumed it was diving for the jugular. I lashed out with both arms, trying to bat it away. I missed, but the grouse backed off, and I hurried down the trail. It apparently accepted my tactical withdrawal as victory and did not pursue.

But the mosquitoes did—for three more stinging, wicked miles until I found the dreamed-of palisade and the salving breeze did indeed waft them all away. I lingered there for some time, savoring lunch, the view, and the sweet feeling of nothing crawling on my skin. I assumed I was also safe from the grouse. I mused upon the fact that wildlife had amazed me once again.

The habits of animals, we're told, are governed by instinct. This is no doubt true, and also fortunate. Imagine what they'd think of us if they could think. It would probably be scandalous and unfit for human consumption. Venison would probably acquire a bitter taste.

Instinct used to be a nebulous concept, difficult to define to anyone's satisfaction. However, now that the Computer Age has dawned (at least according to the folks who design and sell computers), we've been provided with an apt metaphor to delineate instinct from thought. It goes like this: Think of a brain, any brain, as wiring, electronic circuitry. Think of a mind, whatever that is, as software, something which can be programmed. An animal is "hard-wired," meaning the functions of its brain cannot be altered in any significant way. Humans, on the other hand, can conceptualize, engage in abstractions, mentally change and adapt, and, if they deem any of it worthwhile, pass the whole mess along to other humans with compatible software.

Any of us would be horrified to imagine we are programmed in any way, though Madison Avenue would probably take a more sanguine view. In any case, let's say this: Animals, and more specifically here, wildlife, are wired into certain mental patterns at birth. As a result, we can almost always predict what they're going to do. Almost. That wiring sometimes seems more complex and surprising than we would expect. Consider the following encounters.

Everyone else was already bundled up in their sleeping bags, but I was sitting by the campfire, watching it slowly die. It was July, but there on the shore of Lake Superior, the summer night had a chilly bite to it, and the warmth of the fire felt good. The dark expanse of the lake, its water cold and calm, mirrored the constellations. The surrounding forest was restless with birds, insects, and other creatures of the night, and their combined chirps, cries, and rustlings created a softly humming backdrop for the gentle evening. I was serenely poking at the fire, lost in random thoughts, when I sensed another presence. I looked up and was startled to see a fox. It was sitting on its haunches directly across from me, poised on the edge of the circle of light cast by the fire. From no more than twelve feet away it stared at me in motionless silence, its eyes reflecting the fire like two bright sparks. I stared back, afraid to move lest I scare it away. For several seconds our eyes were locked across the low flames; mine wide with wonder, its narrowed in . . . what?

Then one of my companions noisily stirred in his sleep and the fox disappeared, evaporating silently into the dark. For a moment I wondered if I hadn't dozed off and dreamed it. But no, it was real, the fox had been there; I could see tracks. During a brief lapse in the usual order of things, we'd shared the fire and the night. Why had it come so close? Was it panhandling, seeking a handout like the squirrels and the jays? What of that ancient bit of lore about wild animals being deathly afraid of fire? The fox had crouched there, tense but clearly not intimidated. Some would say it had been attracted by the smell of our recent dinner, but who knows? Maybe it was curious about a nocturnal stranger huddled quietly by a fire.

Whatever the reason, the fox was a gift—a gift of the wilderness night and a rare glimpse at the vital force of nature. For I had seen my campfire glimmering in two dark jewels, reflecting intelligence. In those gleaming eyes I had seen the life of the forest: the cunning of the hunter, the wisdom of the prey, the tangled woodland and web of leaves and fur and sunlight.

Another time, on a warm September night in the canoe country along the Minnesota-Ontario border, I found it difficult to remain in the tent. I knew there weren't very many warm nights left, and it seemed a shame not to be out under the stars. I crawled out of the tent at about 2 A.M., unable, or rather unwilling, to sleep. The moon was full, radiant, and riding high, and its reflection in the placid water of Shell Lake was undisturbed. Without a hint of a breeze to play music in the pines, I could clearly hear the low roaring of Devil's Cascade, a stretch of rapids about two miles to the west. It was literally the only sound. The sky was bright and the air so mild, I felt no need for a fire. Besides, the striking of a match would have been horrendously loud.

I crouched on the bedrock of the small island, noting that it was still comfortably charged with the heat of the previous afternoon. I sat quietly, bemused by the moonlit and ethereal landscape of shimmering water and silhouetted pines. Suddenly I heard a sound, a rush of air like a gust of wind. I looked up and saw a shadowy form diving at me from the top of a tree. In a reflexive spasm of self-defense, I raised my hands to cover my head, and the eerie shape pulled up and darted off to the side. It was an owl.

That's funny, I thought. That owl was either extremely hungry or remarkably nearsighted. I supposed it had been confused by some odd reflection or other trick of moonlight. Surely an owl would not consider a human to be fair game. But no, apparently that owl (it looked like a barred owl, a midsized bird) was just really famished and ambitious, because after about two or three minutes it attacked me again. Swooping down out of the same pine, with its deadly talons splayed in menacing anticipation, it gave me a rabbit's-eye view of doomsday. I was amazed, and a little frightened. It was something out of the *Twilight Zone.* One assault was a fluke. A second? That owl obviously meant to sink its claws into my flesh. I jumped to my feet to show the owl how big I am (like a cobra expanding its hood) and waved my arms. Again the misguided predator dodged away, and I figured that would be the end of the episode for certain.

Still, nervous now and fully alert, I followed its flight and saw where it came to rest, perched in a tree near its original roost, and within striking distance. I sat down, keeping my eyes fixed on it. To my astonishment, it made a third pass. I saw it drop from the tree branch, its wings extended, its talons outstretched, its eyes riveted on the quarry. I grabbed a stick, leaped to one side, and threw it at the diving bird. The makeshift flak came nowhere near its target, but the owl was impressed nevertheless, and I saw it fly off over the lake to the trees on the mainland and out of sight. I was left in peace, but I took it as a sign and crawled back into the tent where humans belong.

Garrison Keillor once said that he figured during deer season in Minnesota, when the forests are filled with wandering humans dressed in orange and red, most of the deer climb aboard charter buses and head for Minneapolis. Well, it's no more farfetched than a lot of deer stories I've heard (particularly on Opening Day down at the tavern), and it neatly accounts for the lack of success of many hunters. The point is that the more you observe animals, the more you develop a respect for their wiring. For instance, my dog is my buddy, but whenever I order old "Rover" around, I keep in mind that his brain is related to that of a fox who shared my campfire, and to that of an owl who decided I looked delicious.

SEVENTEEN
October Tale

There was something dead in the woods. From the dirt road I could see three ravens perched at the top of aspen saplings. Three more of the large black scavengers circled overhead, hoarsely croaking. No doubt there were more on the ground, feeding. A flock would not gather for a dead rabbit; there was something big in there.

What kind of carcass would draw so many ravens? Deer? Moose? Bear? Or, you had to wonder . . . human? It was early October and there were hunters in the woods. This was wild country, isolated and often unforgiving.

The birds were only about a quarter mile back into the forest, and an old two-track logging trail, partially overgrown, snaked off through the brush and trees toward the feast. I knew the trail, so I moved along quickly, skirting thorny blackberry bushes that picked and clutched at my jeans. I kept an eye out for fresh tracks in the bare spots, but saw none. After a quarter mile or so the trail widened into a small clearing, an old timber landing taken over by grass and weeds.

The ravens were about 150 feet off to the left, and I surprised them. They exploded out of the woods, beating aloft with wild black flapping and raucous cawing, angry and loud. I counted ten of them. I fixed an eye on the aspens which had served as roosts, assuming the body would lie directly below. They were about 100 feet from the edge of the clearing, poking out of a thick stand of young jack pine.

I waded into the pines, which were just a little taller than me, struggling to keep the perches in sight. The ravens had flown off, their calls faint in the distance. In a few moments I broke into a grove of aspens and expectantly scanned the ground. Nothing. I looked at the tops of the trees. Were these the right ones? It seemed so. Perhaps the birds had not been perching that near to the kill.

I began to circle through the aspens slowly, studying the ground on either side. Most of the leaves had already fallen, and an early snow, wet and heavy, had flattened the dried-out ferns and grasses before melting. The woods were open and naked, and a large carcass should be fairly easy to find. Every few steps I stopped, carefully looking all around, and sniffing the air. The air was cool, about 50 degrees, but perhaps I could still catch a warning whiff of putrefaction. It would be unpleasant to stumble over a corpse.

Suddenly there was a rapid thumping directly overhead. I glanced up, startled. A huge raven was banking away to the north, its wing feathers splayed to catch the southeasterly breeze. It was only a yard or so above the treetops and had a wingspan of close to three feet. As it zoomed off, the black head swiveled, aiming at me with its long sharp beak and a dark beady eye. It issued a guttural squawk and was gone.

I took a few more steps and then another raven swooped in from the south, gliding past only twenty-five feet overhead, and crying when it saw me. Yes, the intruder was still here. I was being watched.

And I was puzzled. Where was the carcass? Surely there must be one; the ravens appeared anxious to return. I sat down and huddled into a clump of hazel brush. Maybe if I hid for a while the birds would forget about me and return to the feast, pinpointing its location. I stayed motionless in the brush, staring at the gray sky through bare branches. A squirrel chattered nearby, and a few remaining leaves rattled in the wind. After only a few minutes in my "blind," a third raven sailed into my field of vision from the east. It was low and slow, its head pivoting from side to side. I held my breath, tensed into utter stillness. The black body was two feet long, ending in the characteristic diamond-shaped tail feathers. The great wings sideslipped a little in the breeze. As it drew abreast of my position the raven's head cocked toward me, and the beak opened to emit a short, raspy *yawp*. It then peeled away, flapping off to the north. I'd been seen. I was being circled and hunted. Would I try to steal their carrion? Or was I regarded as merely another potential meal?

A few years before, on a mild day in February, I'd been skiing across a frozen lake, our old golden retriever valiantly trying to keep up. I wasn't going too fast for him; the trouble was that snow kept crunching up between his toes, causing him to limp. Every fifty yards or so he had to stop, lie down, and clean his paws with his teeth and tongue. He hadn't been limping for more than two or three minutes when two ravens materialized overhead, circling. When the elderly dog stopped to lick his toes, the birds immediately dropped lower and were joined by a third scavenger. Apparently the hobbling dog was worth the wait. By the time we got off the lake, about fifteen minutes later, four ravens had the hapless old retriever pegged for dead.

I thought of him as the third raven disappeared. They were keen-eyed and patient, and it was obviously impossible to conceal myself among the naked aspen and hazel. I headed back to the dense jack pine and crawled under two especially bushy trees which grew side by side. I settled in among the needles, forsaking a view of the sky in favor of total camouflage. If I got comfortable and laid low, perhaps hiding might yet work. There had to be a large carcass in these woods.

But no sooner had I consolidated my new position than I heard a loud and rough beating of wings, seemingly right over my head. Then *caw, caw,* I was seen again. I heard a soft whoosh of air as the raven banked away. I was cautiously crawling to a new tree when another raven soared over, called out, and disappeared. There was no place to hide. I abandoned my covert activity and stalked out of the pines. Surely my dead quarry was somewhere in the aspens. If I couldn't fool the ravens, I'd simply have to quarter the area more diligently until I found it. I started back through the aspen grove, going farther south than before. As I searched, I climbed a small hill that gave me a better view of the immediate surroundings.

I paused to survey the area, and a raven flew in from the east. I was in plain sight on the hilltop, watching it come in, and no doubt it saw me. But as it crossed in front, winging over the base of the hill, it swiveled its head to the north, pointing its beak at the jack pines I'd just left. It made no sound. In less than a minute another bird drifted in from the east, riding a gust. Dipping its right wing, it sideslipped to the north and glided over the pines. For only a moment, just before it flapped away, its head was cocked straight down, looking at the ground. It appeared to be the same spot the other raven had checked out.

Then I saw them—a half dozen aspen saplings growing in the midst of the pines, about a hundred feet away. Both ravens had flown over the little grove. Those must be the trees I'd seen from the road. I'd missed them the first time through the pines, getting into a different clump of aspen. I rushed down the hill and through the jacks, and as I brushed the last bough out of the way, there, at last, was the carcass.

It was a seven-point buck—a magnificent animal that must have gone over two hundred pounds alive. Even in gory death it was beautiful. The coat was thick, even, lustrous; the rack elegant and imposing; the legs charged with inherent grace. The deer was lying on his right side, cushioned by a carpet of leaves. His front limbs were bent at a gentle angle beneath his chest, as if he'd been kneeling when he died. In contrast, his hind legs were twisted all akimbo at unnatural angles—painful just to look at.

The ravens had been hard at work, and the entire anatomy of

the buck was exposed. The rib cage was open to the air, and behind the bloody bones I could see the heart and esophagus. The abdominal cavity was a wet mass of greenish tissue slopping over onto the ground. The left eye had been plucked out and flies were scuttling in and out of the empty socket. But there were relatively few flies around, due, no doubt, to the autumn weather.

What had killed this fine animal, an exemplar of his race? Grasping the antlers, I lifted the head off the ground so I could examine the other eye. It was closed, but I could open the eyelid easily with my fingers. The eyeball was still lifelike, soft and moist. It seemed unlikely the deer had been dead for more than a day or a day and a half, and the carcass had not been moved from where it fell.

My first thought was an arrow. Bow-hunting season was open, and maybe the buck had been wounded, chased, and then later died. Clutching the hind legs, I hoisted the body and partially rolled it over, but there was no trace of an arrow or an arrow wound. Still, as disheveled as the carcass was, it would be impossible to find a wound without the actual arrow. Poachers were a possibility, and there might be a bullet embedded somewhere in the rotting tissues, but I wasn't about to start digging.

We were relatively near to the road, and though it was not heavily traveled, the deer might have been hit by a car and fatally injured, with just enough life left to stumble to that spot. But the legs were unscarred, and surely they would've been struck.

Though there was a wolf pack in the area, it didn't look like a wolf kill. The buck was still basically in one piece, and the bones I could see were ungnawed. I slowly circled the carcass, low to the ground, looking for tracks, scat, or other sign. I painstakingly worked my way out to a fifteen-foot radius around the buck, but all I found were tufts of his hair and dozens of splatters of white raven droppings.

Perhaps he'd died of "natural" causes, something mundane

like old age. I parted his lips and examined his teeth. They didn't look worn at all, but rather young and healthy. His death would remain a mystery.

A raven dove by, squawking, and I felt a pang of resentment. This once regal stag was now raven bait, a meal for flies and worms. It's no wonder that in the mythology of many primitive peoples the raven was a link to evil prophecies and death, a black messenger associated with the night. In its prime, this buck could have held a wolf pack at bay with antlers and slashing hooves; or outrun any danger with breathtaking leaps through dense forest. But you cannot outrun the ravens.

I stood for several minutes, paying last respects; imagining his speed, strength, and savvy; admiring the splendid rack. Those antlers had regenerated for the last time. That particular cycle of rebirth was finished. It didn't seem right. I left, and from back on the dirt road I could see six ravens circling and descending.

I waited four days and then returned. The birds were long gone, but other carrion eaters had dropped by. All that remained were scattered pieces of chewed-up hide and bones. But about thirty-five feet from where the carcass had been, I found the skull and the beautiful antlers. I shall keep them from the scavengers.

And in the meantime there are forests to hunt and trails to rechart. There is wolf song to hear and auroras to rave about. There are gardens to harvest and northern pike to meet. There is a house to finish. And all to be shared.

There are fire calls to answer on subzero nights. There are long months of short, cold days. There are losses to endure, and even though the ravens must eventually die, I doubt they'll ever starve. And all is to be shared.